DIGITAL WORKPLACE STRATEGY & DESIGN

A step-by-step guide to
an empowering employee experience

Oscar Berg & Henrik Gustafsson

English translation
David Friedman

English copyediting
Janet Feenstra

TABLE OF CONTENTS

unicorntitans.com

© Oscar Berg & Henrik Gustafsson 2018
Publisher: Unicorn Titans AB, Sweden
Print: BoD – Books on Demand, Norderstedt, Germany
ISBN: 978-91-984700-4-8

Oscar Berg (co-author) is an internationally acclaimed expert, speaker, and author on topics including social collaboration, digitalization, and the future of work. He heads Unicorn Titans, a Swedish digital innovation agency.
Website: oscarberg.net

Henrik Gustafsson (co-author) is a digital strategist and business developer at Knowit Experience with a focus on productivity, collaboration, and innovation. He also runs MovingMind, which provides coaching in health, energy, and personal development.
Website: movingmind.se/henrikgustafsson/

David Friedman (translator) tailors Swedish messages for international target groups as a translator, copywriter, and copyeditor at Friedman Strategic Copy AB. In addition to financial reports and websites, he specializes in IT with a focus on digitalization.
Website: friedmanstrategiccopy.com

Janet Feenstra (copyeditor) has an established track record editing academic and corporate publications. She is formally trained in copyediting and strategic communication with an MA in English. This is one of a number of books on digitalization in her editing portfolio.
Website: janet-feenstra.com

PREFACE

"Processes—the engines of flux—are now more important than products. Our greatest invention in the past 200 years was not a particular gadget or tool but the invention of the scientific process itself. Once we invented the scientific method, we could immediately create thousands of other amazing things we could have never discovered any other way. This methodical process of constant change and improvement was a million times better than inventing any particular product, because the process generated a million new products over the centuries since we invented it. Get the ongoing process right and it will keep generating ongoing benefits. In our new era, processes trump products."

The quotation above is from *The Inevitable*,[1] a book by Kevin Kelly, who achieved fame as the founder and former executive editor of *Wired* magazine. In our view, it does a good job of summarizing what we need to focus on for successful digitalization and digital transformation of an organization. In addition to a clear purpose and vision, digitalization needs a process that spans the entire organization throughout its life, both creating change and changing when required.

Digitalization also requires a new approach in comparison to how most organizations have previously viewed the use of information technology. With digitalization, new digital technology is harnessed to enable and support new needs and behaviors. These needs and behaviors are in turn impacted and shaped by the digital technology we use. Technological progress and changes in our behavior are inseparable, like two sides of the same coin.

---

1   Kevin Kelly, *The Inevitable: Understanding the 12 Technological Forces That Will Shape Our Future* (Penguin Book, 2017).

THE BLIND SPOT OF DIGITALIZATION

Technological progress is accelerating, and we will see a constant emergence of new digital opportunities and needs that organizations either play a part in creating or must adapt to. In other words, they need to be more innovative and agile.

These demands ultimately trickle down to the employees as individuals and as groups, and they are often caught in between rising demands and a digital work environment that slows them down rather than empowering them. This is because the growth of the digital workplace was almost entirely organic without any holistic view or coordination, making it complex, fragmented, and difficult to use. The question of how this environment should be designed to suit the employees and the work they need to do has not been asked often enough.

In our view, the digital work environment and the employee experience are the blind spots of the ongoing digitalization process.

Digital ways of working that allow unlimited digital communication and collaboration are an absolute must for successful digitalization and the required transformation of an organization and its business. Despite this, we still invest far too little in the digitalization of the employees' ways of working and the development of the digital work environment, at least relative to what is invested in digitalizing the customer experience. And the focus that is dedicated to customers and improving their experience is almost nonexistent for employees.

Customer experience (CX) is often defined as the customer's perception of a brand or organization resulting from all interactions during their relationship. Likewise, the same principle can be applied to employees' perception of the organization they work for – employee experience (EX). This is based on all interactions between the employee and the organization during their employment relationship.

Organizations across all industries must provide the best possible employee experience to remain competitive. Succeeding in this will help them attract and retain talent, enhance employee engagement and productivity, and contribute to a better customer experience. The importance of the user experience in maximizing the value of using digital services is akin to the key role of the employee experience for the value created by employees individually and collectively. This necessitates working smarter together to maximize value creation in line with the organization's purpose.

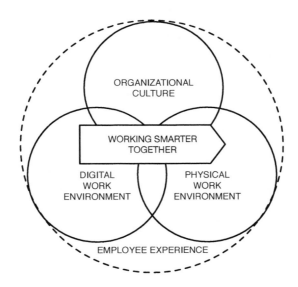

Similar to the different aspects of employee experience presented by Jacob Morgan in his book *The Experience Advantage*,[2] we see the employee experience as comprising three parts: the organizational culture, the digital work environment, and the physical work environment (see illustration above). The employee experience is the sum of all these parts, and each must interact seamlessly and leverage each other to enable and empower employees to work smarter together.

---

2   Jacob Morgan, *The Employee Experience Advantage - How to Win the War for Talent by Giving Employees the Workspaces They Want, the Tools They Need, and a Culture They Can Celebrate* (Wiley, 2017).

The continuing digitalization of our society and of our professional and personal lives steadily increases the importance of the digital work environment and its resulting impact on the entire employee experience. Our digital interactions shape our culture – the ideas and social behaviors we have in common. More specifically, we have a need to digitally interact with each other from anywhere, and this dictates what we require from our physical work environments and how we interact with them.

HOW TO USE THIS BOOK

This book presents an approach for holistically designing a digital work environment that considers both the culture and the physical work environment. Use the overview of the book's structure below to quickly find the knowledge you need when you need it.

Chapter one introduces you to how digitalization is changing the business environment, why it is important to support creative knowledge work and develop digital ways of working, and what type of problems many employees encounter in their digital work environment.

Chapter two defines the digital workplace and describes what approach organizations need to both address problems in their employees' digital work environment and take advantage of new digital opportunities.

Chapter three explains servicification and service-dominant logic as applied to the development of the digital workplace, defines key concepts, and illustrates service orientation.

Chapter four describes how to quickly outline a vision and roadmap for the digital workplace and align them with the organization's strategies by using an iterative and inclusive strategy process, which also enables new digital opportunities to be identified and utilized.

Chapter five sets the stage for how to go from digital workplace strategy to the design of digital services. It explains how to plan service development and how to design the right services in the right way using the principles and tools of service design.

We conclude with a short **epilogue** where we share some personal reflections and a few tips on how we can help you on your continuing journey.

In the back, you will find a list of **references** and an **index** with key terms to help you navigate the book.

When we began writing this book, our goal was to share a pragmatic value-centric and user-centric process for digitalization that is characterized by a holistic view, which we saw was clearly missing in the development of digital work environments. This is why we chose to fill this gap with the approach, processes, and methodology born out of our years as consultants, which we actively continue to develop and refine.

We hope that this book will help you and your organization create a digital workplace and an employee experience that truly empowers people.

Henrik Gustafsson and Oscar Berg

CHAPTER 1

DRIVERS
& CHALLENGES

1.1   INTRODUCTION

The rapid digitalization of our society is fundamentally changing the playing field for how companies and organizations create value for their customers. With the internet and social media, the power wielded by companies to influence which products and services become successful is shifting to consumers. At the same time, the increasing use of digital services in our personal lives causes us to develop new behaviors and expectations, and companies are struggling to keep up.

The gap that emerges between our increasing expectations and the inability of companies to meet them is ripe for new challengers. Those who see and are able to seize the opportunities of new behaviors, new technology, and new ways of creating value can quickly knock the wind out of previously successful companies by utilizing new innovations and business models. These new challengers can come from unexpected places, and neither they nor consumers care about old industry dividing lines anymore.

As a result, it is now nearly impossible for a company to make long-term plans for its business in any great detail. Instead, it must be change-ready and able to quickly adjust its offering and customer touchpoints. It must also identify in what direction the market, customer behavior, and technology are heading and adapt to new conditions rapidly. This requires that organizations be responsive, collaborative, creative, and agile – but many have failed to make these a priority.

1.1.1   DIGITAL TRANSFORMATION

Most organizations need to make a fundamental change – digital transformation. However, rather than investing in digital technology and purchasing new systems, this entails thinking digitally from the ground up and placing both customers and employees and their experience at the heart of everything the organization does.

Digital transformation means looking for and utilizing the possibilities unlocked by digital technologies to create the most value and the best experience possible for customers, employees, and other stakeholders involved in the business.

> *A corporation is a living organism; it has to continue to shed its skin. Methods have to change. Focus has to change. Values have to change. The sum total of those changes is transformation.*[1]

– Andy Grove, former chairman and CEO of Intel

Creating a positive customer experience has become an increasingly important competitive factor. The entire organization must engage its customers and make the customer touchpoints with the organization and its products and services as smooth as possible. It also needs to *continuously improve* the customer experience. This requires collecting data and feedback from customers about their experience and using this to achieve new insight into how the organization's value proposition to its customers and the customer experience can be improved overall. These are then used to make the changes needed to improve the value proposition and customer experience. This ongoing process is illustrated in Figure 1.

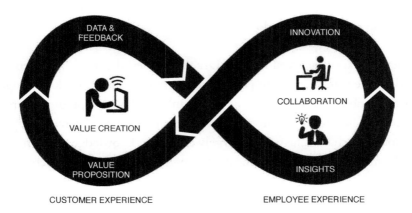

Figure 1. The continuous loop for customer and employee experience development.

---

1   Mike Sager, "Andy Grove: What I've Learned," *Esquire*, January 29, 2007, https://www.esquire.com/entertainment/interviews/a1449/learned-andy-grove-0500/.

Accomplishing this quickly and effectively requires the organization's employees to excel at collaborating throughout the organization, from customer service to product development and then back to sales and marketing. It is simply not enough for the customer experience to be digital – the employee experience is equally important.

Working and collaborating digitally is the only way to achieve the agility, reach, flexibility, and collective capability required. Just as steam was crucial to powering the Industrial Revolution, the internet and digital technology are also crucial to organizations that want to be successful going forward. Therefore, digital technology must be at the heart of everything they do.

1.1.2   THE CHANGING NATURE OF WORK

The content and nature of human work is in the process of dramatic change as a result of rapid technological progress. A shift from manual work to knowledge work has been underway since the start of industrialization, and machines have increasingly taken over more of the manual work. Today, many employees work on planning, organizing, managing, and improving the business instead. On the basis of the data available, along with their own knowledge and that of others, they create information that is then communicated to and used by others. This is what knowledge workers do.

When management guru Peter F. Drucker coined the term "knowledge worker", he was referring to people whose main asset is their knowledge. It's their job to think, and among their ranks are lawyers, programmers, engineers, architects, and researchers. Today, new types of careers keep cropping up that exclusively or largely engage in knowledge work in the form of complex communications, analytical reasoning, and creative thinking.

The automation of routine knowledge work is another change that appears highly likely to have major consequences for the future. Computers and software are now taking over increasingly more routine knowledge work just as routine manual work has largely been replaced by machines and robots. The diagram in Figure 2 illustrates this change by showing the shift from routine to non-routine work in the US economy from the mid-1970s.

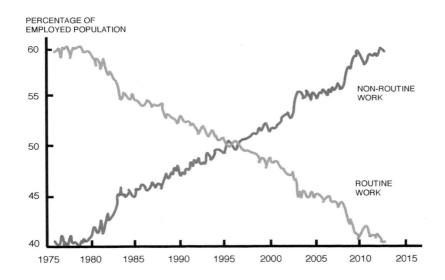

PERCENTAGE OF
EMPLOYED POPULATION

Figure 2. The polarization from routine work to non-routine work.[2]

The increasing rate of digitalization based on the internet as a platform and the emergence of new technologies like virtual and augmented reality, the Internet of Things, and artificial intelligence accelerate this trend. We are already seeing "robot journalists" report sports scores for the Associated Press,[3] and in the US, "robot lawyers" currently offer legal assistance faster and cheaper than human lawyers can.

2   Stefania Albanesi, Victoria Gregory, Christina Patterson, and Ayşegül Şahin, "Is Job Polarization Holding Back the Labor Market?," *Liberty Street Economics*, March 27, 2013, http://libertystreeteconomics.newyorkfed.org/2013/03/is-job-polarization-holding-back-the-labor-market.html.

3   Ross Miller, "AP's 'robot journalists' are writing their own stories now," *The Verge*, Jan 29, 2015, https://www.theverge.com/2015/1/29/7939067/ap-journalism-automation-robots-financial-reporting.

However, one category of human work that is gaining both in scope and significance is creative and collaborative knowledge work. This category is shown in the upper-right quadrant of Figure 3. This work demands typical human qualities and capabilities such as empathy, creativity, improvisation, and collaboration, and we must all develop these to stay relevant on the labor market.

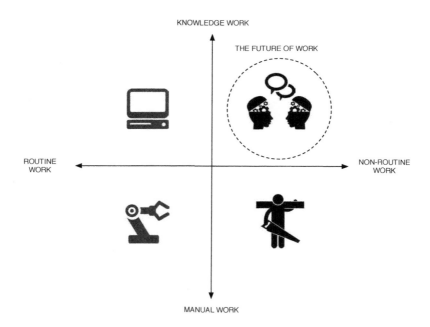

Figure 3. The future of work is creative knowledge work and creative manual work.

1.1.3   ENGAGEMENT FUELS PRODUCTIVITY

Most large organizations today have structured and optimized their business to mass produce products and services in a relatively stable and predictable world. They chased higher returns on their owners' investments, mainly by increasing cost efficiency and creating economies of scale, but this was often at the expense of the people who worked there. Human qualities such as the ability to scrutinize and take initiative were viewed as merely getting in the way of production at the time.

In a sense, the crowning accomplishment of the Hierarchy and its management processes is the enterprise on autopilot, everyone ideally situated as a cog whirring on a steady, unthinking and predictable machine.

– John Kotter, Konosuke Matsushita Professor of Leadership, Emeritus at the Harvard Business School

Now these organizations suddenly find themselves completely dependent on access to creative knowledge workers – those who scrutinize prior assumptions and solutions – in their search for new ways to create value for customers. The knowledge workers often encounter an organization with assumptions about its business that do not apply to creative knowledge work. Another issue is that these organizations do not understand what motivates employees to do their best or what modern leadership entails.

Therefore, the companies and organizations of today and tomorrow must get better at recruiting, developing, and retaining knowledge workers with the right attitudes, qualities, and skills. The employees must be given the right conditions and support to do their best and feel engaged in their work. Studies in recent decades have shown a clear link between a high level of employee engagement and organizational success.

It doesn't make sense to hire smart people and then tell them what to do; we hire smart people so they can tell us what to do.[4]

– Steve Jobs, founder and former CEO of Apple

Paradoxically, other studies show a trend where employees are becoming increasingly less engaged, and this applies to large organizations in particular. Aside from costing them heavily in lost production, this is a sign that something is fundamentally wrong with how they operate (Figure 4).

---

4   Shahrzad Rafati, "What Steve Jobs taught executives about hiring," Fortune, 2015, http://fortune.com/2015/06/09/shahrzad-rafati-keeping-your-best-employees/.

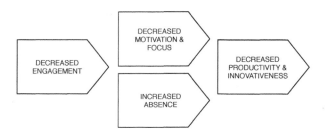

Figure 4. The degree of engagement affects productivity and innovativeness.

There are naturally many reasons for this, but essentially it involves the ability, or perhaps the inability, of the organization to transition from routine work to creative knowledge work. A key part of this transition is to design the digital workplace to support creative and collaborative knowledge work and boost its employees' engagement in the business.

1.1.4   WE WORK THE SAME AS IN 1995

For collaborative work, the time is long gone when it was possible to gather everyone in the same room. Today, we need to be able to work when and where it needs to be done, and the same goes for collaboration. Here's where digital tools and ways of working come into play.

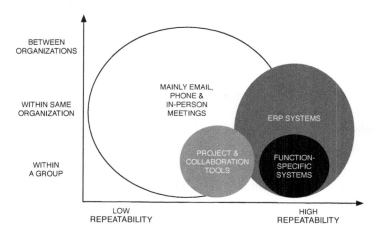

Figure 5. Support for creative and collaborative knowledge work is often lacking.

Most organizations have implemented IT systems that support repeatable business processes such as purchasing, manufacturing, sales, and distribution. In addition, they often have tools for management, communication, and collaboration within small groups such as project teams. However, there is a gap in terms of tools that support creative and collaborative knowledge work, as illustrated in Figure 5.

If an organization has social collaboration tools, they tend to become isolated islands not integrated with the other parts of the digital work environment. Its social collaboration tools also fail to replace well-established ways of working based on email, meetings, and phone calls, even in cases where they are significantly better-suited for these tasks. As a result, the cognitive load on employees increases rather than decreases. Thus, when new tools are introduced to support new ways of working, it's important to remove the old ones.

In some sense, many organizations work the same way as they did in 1995. They still use the tools and ways of working that began to emerge at that time. Not much has happened since then apart from that these ways and tools spread from just a few employees to all the employees (see Figure 6).

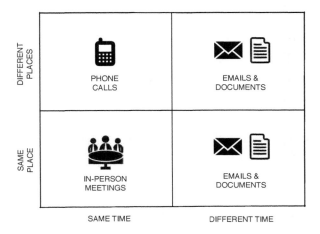

Figure 6. The dominant modes of communication and collaboration.

However, reality was completely different in 1995 when compared with today. This makes these ways of working hopelessly outdated and inefficient.

1.2   WORK ENVIRONMENT PROBLEMS

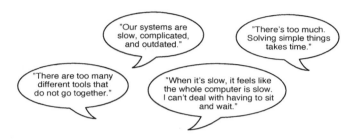

Figure 7. Authentic voices about their digital work environment.

Although the systems and tools put in place for the employees were intended to make them more efficient and productive, many feel frustrated and that their hands are tied by the very systems and tools meant to help them. This causes enormous stress, and in some cases, even results in illness and sick leave. And "office work" isn't the only type of work where the digital work environment causes frustration, stress, and sick leave. It can be even worse for those who work "on the floor".

Inevitably, our work environments are becoming increasingly digital. Digitalization affects everyone everywhere, regardless of whether you are a system developer, payroll administrator, line manager, nurse, teacher, service technician, or sales clerk, and you will increasingly use digital devices and tools in your day-to-day work. Your ways of working will be digitized, and you will embrace this to create more value for the customers or citizens you serve.

The digitalization of our ways of working and our work environments is designed to make us more productive and innovative, thus raising the quality of what we do. The paradox is that the digital work environment is often not inviting, not engaging, and does not raise capacity in the manner required to support this.

We are forced to struggle with an increasingly large number of complex systems that are difficult to use, and we are overwhelmed by the sheer volume of information via email and other information channels. At the same time, our work is becoming more unpredictable, demanding, complex, and subject to change than ever before, yet we are expected to be creative, collaborative, and flexible.

And there's no way to "digitally detox" by briefly disconnecting and relaxing at work either – it's quite the opposite. Work is inevitably becoming increasingly digitalized, and we cannot do our jobs if we are not constantly connected, logged in, and glued to our computers or tablets. Shutting down an entire digital work environment or even individual systems obviously cannot be done in practice – the business would come to a standstill. Instead, something needs to be done to improve the situation. Otherwise, there is a risk it will grow worse as the implementation of IT systems continues along the same old track. We need to identify the most common problems and understand their causes before we can act.

Our experience tells us that most problems that crop up can be grouped into several general categories, which are illustrated in Figure 8 and described in the following section.

COMPLEXITY   FRAGMENTATION   INFLEXIBILITY   REDUNDANCY   INCONSISTENCY   POOR USABILITY

Figure 8. General categories for digital work environment problems.

1.2.1   COMPLEXITY

Just a few decades ago, employees generally had relatively few systems and tools. However, increasingly more processes and tasks have been digitalized over time. Thus, the number of systems and tools employees are expected to use and are required to keep up with has also increased. Their implementation has rarely been coordinated, and they have not been uniformly designed, which further increases the complexity of the digital work environment.

This struggle is validated by a report from the Swedish Work Environment Authority,[5] which reviewed international research on digital work environments. The report concludes that some occupational groups use as many as 20–30 systems and that, despite this, new IT systems are regularly implemented without first establishing their needs. Jonas Söderström cites as an example that the Karolinska Institute University Library in Stockholm, Sweden, has 117 systems for only 110 employees.[6] Another study found the following as a result of the implementation of new IT solutions without a focus on how this affects individual employees:

> *"The effective usage rates of enterprise software are down compared to two years ago, with users experiencing productivity losses of around 17%. It's like giving everyone Friday off."* [7]

1.2.2   INFLEXIBILITY

The digital work environment of many organizations was originally created to support traditional desk work. At the time, it involved digitizing analog information and data. Typewriters were replaced with computers and printers, and internal mail was replaced with email. Work was performed in front of a screen at a desk in an office.

---

5   *Oklarheter kring den digitala arbetsmiljön* (Arbetsmiljöverket, 2016), https://www.av.se/press/oklarheterkringden-digitala-arbetsmiljon/.

6   Jonas Söderström, *Arbetsmiljöombud Vision, Göteborg 8 okt 2015* (Slideshare, 2015), http://www.slideshare.net/Jonas_inUse/arbetsmiljoombud-vision-gteborg-8-okt-2015.

7   *IT Adoption Insight Report* (Neochange, 2012)

Now the situation is totally different. As knowledge workers, employees need to be able to work from various locations when and where the work needs to be done. People in almost all careers need to be able to use digital technology to perform their work. Many will never sit at a desk in an office because they perform their work elsewhere. On a factory floor. In a store. In a classroom. Or next to a patient in a treatment room. This development poses completely new requirements in terms of flexibility and access to relevant digital services. Unfortunately, the digital work environment does not always meet these requirements, and the problem is not just technology. In many organizations, people are stuck in old structures, approaches, ways of working, and behaviors that are difficult to break out of.

1.2.3   FRAGMENTATION

The increase in specialization in both the private and public sectors has significantly boosted the positive productivity trend we have seen over the years. But specialization also has a downside. Many of the IT systems introduced were designed to support specific specialist domains such as HR, finance, and product development. As a result, they perpetuated the organizational silos created by the increase in specialization and made collaboration more difficult across, within, and between organizations.

1.2.4   REDUNDANCY

Many large organizations carry a long legacy of poorly coordinated and integrated IT systems. In many cases, they have the same type of functionality, which makes it difficult to know what should be done and where – and they are paying for the same functionality many times over. For instance, many systems include document management and collaboration functionalities. They may also include the management of basic information about employees and customers. As a result, the information is often spread out across multiple systems and the same information is recreated over and over again.

In addition, most of the content in many organizations is unstructured content, such as documents and websites, which is difficult to process in an effective and controlled manner. This often involves large batches of text contained in documents spread out across local hard drives or file servers, in email systems, on websites, or the intranet. For instance, the moment a document is sent by email, it spreads like a virus and creates even more unnecessary redundancy, which is costly to manage and impairs findability.

1.2.5   INCONSISTENCY

It is often the case that the user experience between different systems in an organization is inconsistent. This applies to not only the systems' appearance but also their functionality. For instance, there may be one way to perform a task in one system and a completely different way to perform a similar task in another system. It is then up to the users to learn the differences and remember them each time they use each system. This increases the cognitive load on the employee, resulting in stress and mistakes.

1.2.6   POOR USABILITY

Until the mid-2000s, IT development was driven entirely by companies and organizations. New IT solutions and computers were introduced in the workplace first. Systems were purchased to support various administrative functions, automate processes, and enhance the governance and monitoring of the business with the aim to increase quality and efficiency. If there were any usability requirements, they were low on the list of priorities. Furthermore, suppliers did not make usability a particularly high priority in the design of their IT systems either. As a result, many organizations are stuck with old IT systems with major usability deficiencies. And although suppliers have gotten better at usability in recent years, they still have a long way to go to catch up with the tools and services designed for consumers. The latter – services designed for consumers – is what sets the employees' level of expectation in terms of usability.

1.3 THE USER EXPERIENCE DEBT

Imagine you have a big family and a large supply of tableware, but the dishwasher is broken, so you decide not to wash the dishes after each meal. From breakfast through to dinner, you accumulate an increasingly larger pile of dishes until your tableware runs out. Now when you go to the kitchen, you are met with an overwhelming pile of dirty dishes. The mere thought of dealing with it stresses you out, so you decide to go and lay down. But when you wake up and go to the kitchen the next morning for your morning coffee, you realize you have no choice but to roll up your sleeves and do the dishes. Of course, when you are done, the cycle starts all over again.

You leave your dirty dishes anxiety at home and go to work, where a new IT system has just been implemented. But it has not been designed in dialogue with you or any of the other intended users. No one has made sure that it is easy and appealing to use or that it looks like any of the other systems you have worked in before. When you use the system, you are frustrated not only with how complex and difficult it is but also how it does not look and behave like other systems. This does not support your work in the way it could at all. Over time, the system grows to include new functionality. But the more systems and functionality that are introduced, the more complex and difficult the digital work environment becomes.

When the gap between an acceptable user experience and the actual user experience grows wider, a *user experience debt* is accumulated, which the user has to carry every day (Figure 9). This is similar to a financial debt that keeps increasing with new loans instead of the original loan being paid off. Eventually, you reach a point where interest payments alone eat up all your purchasing power, and the pressure of the ever-increasing user experience debt ends up draining your work capacity. The user experience debt can reach levels where the digital work environment becomes a serious work environment problem.

Therefore, you need to actively work to "pay off" the debt by making investments in areas such as higher usability, more consistent design across systems, and better integration.

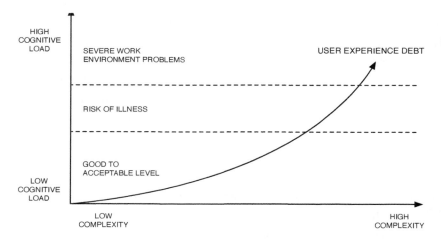

Figure 9. Accumulation of user experience debt.

Unfortunately, many organizations increase their user experience debt faster than they pay it off by implementing new IT systems without putting much thought into those they already have.

1.4   THE CAUSES OF THE PROBLEMS

In our view, the causes of these problems are primarily organizational in nature, specifically the lack of a holistic view, the lack of coordination, and the lack of user focus.

1.4.1   LACK OF A HOLISTIC VIEW AND COORDINATION

In many organizations, each business domain or system owner prioritizes their own goals and needs before what would be best for the organization and business as a whole. For instance, they defend their own systems when they find out the same functionality is included in the systems of other business domains.

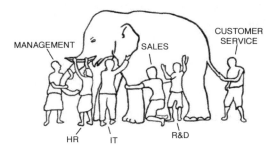

Figure 10. The six blind men and the elephant.

The situation is similar to the Indian story of the six blind men and the elephant (Figure 10). The men feel only their part of the elephant and then tell each other their truth about the elephant, but they end up contradicting each other. Each man only considers the elephant from his own perspective – none of them see the whole. This makes it hard to look after the elephant properly.

The root of the problem to be solved is organizational in nature. IT system providers do not think and act on the basis of what is best for the individual employee or for the organization as a whole. Instead, they think and act based on their organizational and individual areas of responsibility. This is a textbook example of suboptimization and what can happen when we allow an inside-out perspective to dominate. As a result, you end up competing with each other instead of collaborating. The individual parts of the digital work environment overlap and are often in direct conflict with each other.

> *What we need to do is learn to work in the system, by which I mean that everybody, every team, every platform, every division, every component is there not for individual competitive profit or recognition, but for contribution to the system as a whole on a win–win basis.*[8]
>
> – W. Edward Deming, professor, author, and engineer

8   Ray Aldag and Loren Kuzuhara. *Creating High Performance Teams: Applied Strategies and Tools for Managers and Team Members.* Routledge, 2015

The question of ownership naturally comes up in this context. Who takes ownership of so many resources that are intended to meet so many different needs? According to Gartner, 46 percent of all organizations surveyed have a digital workplace initiative in progress, but only four percent have identified an owner and leader of their digital workplace.[9]

So, does someone need to take ownership of the digital workplace? In our opinion – yes, just as someone needs to be responsible for city planning within a city. A lack of ownership of the whole causes many of the problems in the digital workplace, thus making ownership fragmented. Each person owns and is responsible for their part, but no one takes ownership of or feels responsible for ensuring the optimal functioning of the digital work environment as a whole. This is why the digital work environment is often found in such a poor state.

Therefore, an organization without someone to take ownership of its digital workplace can expect a significantly greater risk of failure. Holistic ownership is a key part of the solution. Without this, there is a high risk that the digital workplace will come to a halt at a single initiative instead of developing continuously as a process. Taking ownership for the entire digital workplace may seem both scary and difficult. It's not easy, that's for sure. Nevertheless, someone seeking a challenge with the experience and skills to take it on should not be afraid to do so. In our opinion, this is a significant and meaningful role because the digital workplace is an enabler for the digital transformation of the business.

Some organizations have appointed a special digital workplace committee with representatives from various business domains. In our opinion, this just barely cuts it. The risk is that it ends up a case of "shared responsibility is no responsibility", as the saying goes. Here, we can see the need for both leadership and management by objectives that have been jointly agreed.

---

9   Carol Rozwell and Achint Aggarwal. *Attention to Eight Building Blocks Ensures Successful Digital Workplace Initiatives.* Gartner, 2015

According to Gartner, the Chief Digital Officer (CDO) should be the person to take ownership of the digital workplace, which sounds reasonable to us.[10] The person who leads the digital transformation in an organization is also dependent on there being a digital workplace that enables this transformation. Placing the digital workplace outside of this person's direct control is probably not a good idea, as they are two sides of the same coin.

1.4.2   LACK OF USER FOCUS

No one asked us what we need, which makes it impossible for them to understand our needs.

– Employee of a large organization

Another cause of the problems outlined above is the lack of user focus. Many organizations have a clear technology focus when they procure, develop, and implement IT systems. They have an overly mechanical way of looking at the IT systems' interaction with the business and end up focusing on identifying what functionality is required to support the tasks, activities, and workflows of the business. Rarely do they choose and design systems in the way best suited to the conditions and needs of the user and to help them achieve their goals in a variety of usage situations.

Some say that more than 70 percent of all IT projects fail. A study by Standish for Computerworld surveyed 3555 IT projects between 2003 and 2012 with labor costs of at least $10 million and found that only 6.4 percent of these projects were a success.[11] A failed IT project is usually defined as a project that exceeds its budget, fails to deliver on time, or does not give the client the functions that they were promised.

---

10   Carol Rozwell and Achint Aggarwal, "Attention to Eight Building Blocks Ensures Successful Digital Workplace Initiatives," Gartner, June 15, 2016,

11   Jim Ditmore, "Why Do Big IT Projects Fail So Often? InformationWeek," InformationWeek, October 28, 2013, https://www.informationweek.com/strategic-cio/executive-insights-and-innovation/why-do-big-it-projects-fail-so-often/d/d-id/1112087.

Of course, this is not good. A 2012 study by McKinsey found that 17 percent of IT projects with a budget over $15 million went so badly they posed a threat to these companies' very existence.[12]

The definition of a failed IT project says a lot about the predominant view of IT and how misinformed it is. It tells us that the most important thing is to deliver all the ordered functionalities within the set budget and time frame. There is no mention of delivering business value, such as increased productivity, customer satisfaction, or reduced costs. A project may naturally exceed its budget and schedule without delivering all functions ordered, yet still add business value. Conversely, a project that runs like clockwork and delivers everything the purchaser ordered and only a little bit extra hardly adds any business value. Business value should be the primary metric we assess.

This requires that one acts on the insight that the value of a new IT system is not realized until it is used in the business. It will not create any value at all until it comes into use. All the time and money spent on developing or purchasing the system can be viewed as a sunk cost, as illustrated in Figure 11.

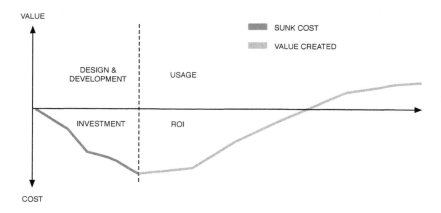

Figure 11. Sunk costs must be compensated through improvements.

12   Charles Roxburgh, Geoffrey Sands, Hugo Sarrazin, James Manyika, Magdalena Westergren, Michael Chui, and Richard Dobbs, *The social economy: Unlocking value and productivity through social technologies* (McKinsey Global Institute: 2012)

Therefore, the organization cannot begin to pay off these costs until the system is implemented in the business and the employees begin to use it. To put it simply, the system must enable a better way of doing something than before. Hopefully, after it has been in use for some time, a gain will be achieved when the cumulative return exceeds the overall investment. But this is far from a sure thing and begs the question, how often does the return actually exceed the investment?

In light of this, it's strange that many organizations invest so much in developing or purchasing systems and relatively little in ensuring they actually improve ways of working and that employees start using them correctly. The work is most often considered complete when a new system goes live, but that is actually when the hard work to make it pay off begins. The organization rarely follows up by measuring whether the gains achieved for the business exceeded the costs lost in terms of volume, that is, if it's even possible to measure this. Why is this the case?

One reason is that IT system implementation projects do not claim responsibility for achieving the desired business impact, only that the system is ready for use. The fact of the matter is that the projects cannot take full responsibility for this because a project always has a beginning and an end within a set budget. The problem is that, once delivered, businesses rarely have the capacity to realize the potential of these projects and thus achieve the desired business impact. People in the organization often go back to business as usual fairly quickly after an IT project is delivered and finalized. Usually, the resources or perseverance are lacking to allow the change process to continue in such a way that the business impact is achieved. After all, people have jobs to do, and business development is seen as something that should be done on the side.

The projects also tend to have a heavy bias toward information technology, which can push aside business goals as well as the users' needs and requirements. The focus is on delivering an IT system with a specific functionality and characteristics within a set time frame and budget. Consequently, "IT projects" is an accurate term for these projects and we should not be misled into believing they are "business development projects".

In addition, the IT projects are often substantial in scope, with long roadmaps and massive deliveries where everything is dumped on the users all at once. This can be compared to slow, overloaded container ships that take a long time to reach port. They have their predetermined routes and experience great difficulty changing course if changes in the surrounding area or other conditions require this. Upon final project delivery, if the project is ever completed at all, it is suddenly expected that large-scale changes will be made immediately in the business. However, the organization and the individual employees may not be capable of fully adopting these changes.

Last but not least, IT projects rarely involve the prospective users in the business – the employees – until it's time for them to start using what has already been implemented . This leads to a couple of very negative consequences:

- The project missed the opportunity to develop a more profound understanding of the prospective users, their needs, and their usage situations, which reduces the likelihood that they developed the right solution and designed it the right way.
- The employees are not prepared for the change and what is required of them, which drastically reduces the likelihood that they will fully embrace it and change their ways of working.

If the prospective users had been involved from the beginning, then they could have influenced the development in a direction that actually meets the right needs in the right way. This also means that they are invested in the solution, see it as their own, and are primed to become ambassadors when it's time to implement it in the business.

1.5   THE CHANGE THAT IS NEEDED

Without doubt, getting out of or avoiding falling into the situation that many organizations find themselves in regarding the digital work environment requires a different way of thinking and working. Yet change is hard, especially when it requires a change in thinking and questioning existing assumptions. So, let's remind ourselves what almost all change theories state about change:

- Change is a process, not an event – the process must be established.
- Change takes time – it requires patience and perseverance.
- Change is social – the right people can have a major impact on how the change is received in the social environment.
- Change is made real by what people do – you have to practice what you preach and be a role model.

1.6   SUMMARY

In this chapter we covered:

- How digitalization is rapidly changing and creating an unpredictable business environment, and how organizations need to respond to this.
- What problems we see in the employees' digital work environment in many organizations as grouped into six categories: complexity, fragmentation, inflexibility, redundancy, inconsistency, and poor usability, and how these increase the user experience debt.
- What we believe are the root causes of the problems – the lack of a holistic view and coordination, and the lack of user focus, which are considerable causes of the failure of most IT projects.

So, how do we approach these challenges and problems while, at the same time, identifying and utilizing digital opportunities?

CHAPTER 2

ADOPTING A NEW APPROACH

2.1   INTRODUCTION

As employees, we now expect digital capabilities and our user experience to be equivalent to what we can get as consumers. We can communicate with anyone in the whole world. We can perform various tasks and meet various needs and preferences via digital services wherever we are via the most suitable device. And the services we use are simple and appealing.

The problem is that many of us consider our digital work environment to be complex, inflexible, and incoherent, with poorly structured systems that are difficult to use. There is a substantial gap between our expectations of what a digital work environment should be and our experience of it in reality. In addition to making our work more difficult, this also causes frustration and saps our motivation. So, why is this the case?

Imagine living and working in a city without the intention or means to organize and structure buildings, streets, and squares as a whole in order to make living and working in the city simple. It could hardly be called a functioning city, and those who could leave would leave.

Yet, our digital work environments have sprung up without the equivalent of urban planning. Countless systems and tools have been designed and implemented independently of one another without considering the employees' perspective, the employees' situation, and the appearance and functioning of the digital work environment through the lens of the employees. As a result, the environment that was intended to make our jobs easier makes our jobs harder instead. The complexity grows with each system and function added, which, paradoxically as it may be, can lead to a decrease in productivity although the individual systems and functions per se are made more powerful. This leads to our view of how the digital workplace should be defined:

A digital work environment designed purposefully and holistically with the user front and center.

Some might disagree with this definition, arguing that it just defines the characteristics of a successful digital workplace. We could have simply defined the digital workplace as "All the digital tools and solutions the employees need to get their work done", but in that case, what would make the digital workplace any different from what most employees already work in? Well, nothing. In addition, when defining it is as a set of tools and solutions, we are inclined to focus too much on the *what* – the technology. We need to break away from a technology-centric mindset to avoid the problems this way of thinking causes. Also, as technology is in constant flux, such a definition can hardly be relied upon for long.

We believe the digital workplace has to be defined in a way that separates it from a digital work environment that has not been designed holistically or with the user front and center. It needs to make clear how we should think and act to get it right. We need to see and understand the entire digital work environment from the point of view of the users in order to design it in a way that empowers them.

Just as in the case of urban planning, the knowledge and intention to structure the whole and ensure that each part interacts well are crucial. The digital work environment must be as effective as possible in meeting every need of its users. This requires both a holistic view and the ability to put the individual user front and center, which in turn, requires a common strategy, coordination, and governance for the entire digital workplace. In addition, policies and guidelines are needed for the appearance, functioning, and development of all its services and characteristics. Every change must be designed to fit well with the employees' digital work environment and with the whole.

We believe that a functioning digital workplace is the foundation for successful digital transformation, as illustrated in Figure 12. The digital workplace serves as the platform needed to enable the organization to rapidly adapt to new expectations, requirements, and opportunities.

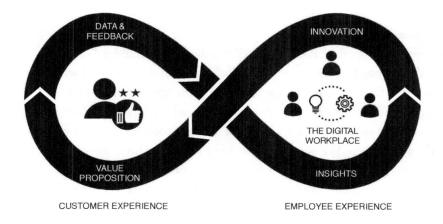

Figure 12. The digital workplace plays a key role in digital transformation.

The development of our digital work environments requires a completely new way of thinking and acting – one that puts the people who work in these environments front and center.

2.2   THE PROCESS IS THE KEY TO SUCCESS

Over the years, many have attempted to understand, and find models to explain, why some companies have such a great capability to be innovative and, time and time again, develop new products and services in areas where they were previously not active.

One of the most popular theories put forth in recent times is Simon Sinek's *Start with Why*.[1] Sinek believes he has found a common denominator among innovative companies and uses Apple as an example. Apple always starts with why it is doing something instead of what it is doing, which is what most companies tend to do.

Sinek's theory is best explained by a model called the "Golden Circle", which consists of three rings:

---

1   Simon Sinek, *Start with Why: How Great Leaders Inspire Everyone to Take Action* (Portfolio, 2011).

WHAT

If we start from the outside, the outer layer of the circle represents what the company does. This is usually easy to describe because it is simply a description of the products or services that the company provides, but it is also easy for other companies to copy it.

HOW

The middle layer describes how the company does what it does, for example, how they produce, present, and sell their products or services as well as how they think about what they do. This is not as easy to work out and then copy.

WHY

The inner layer, the core, represents why the company does what it does. In other words, why the company exists in the first place, what it believes in, what its culture is, and what its values are. This is immensely difficult for other companies to describe and copy.

Sinek discovered that what separates the most successful companies and leaders from those less successful is that they know their purpose and they consistently think, communicate, and act on the basis of that purpose. They are purpose-driven. Companies such as Apple and Google can be considered in this category of companies.

So, why are we bringing up the Golden Circle theory in a book about the digital workplace? Well, because we think that the concepts behind it are also of the utmost relevance for developing the digital workplace. Far too many opinions of the digital workplace are based around an image of countless tools and functionalities. We believe that this leads to an incorrect and ultimately counterproductive way of thinking about and acting on the development of the digital workplace. Functionalities and characteristics will inevitably change over time. After all, few things change as quickly as digital technology. If too much focus is dedicated to the functionality of the digital workplace, we run the risk of getting trapped in a solution-centric and technology-centric focus instead of actively understanding and supporting the business and its goals and needs.

Instead of focusing on what the digital workplace should consist of, we need to start with defining its purpose – what we call its *mission* – and then how it needs to develop to best fulfill this purpose. It is, of course, up to each organization to define the exact purpose of the digital workplace, and it requires a lot of effort to define and align it with its business strategy. Yet, in practice, we believe that it always revolves around supporting new digital ways of working and empowering employees to work smarter together. So, after the purpose has been identified, only one question remains: how should the digital workplace be developed to achieve this?

This is where we see a clear gap between how most organizations work and how they, in a strictly methodical sense, should strive to develop the digital workplace. We go so far as to say that this is the primary cause of not only the poor state of digital work environments in many organizations but also the failure of the desired impact of internal IT investments to materialize. On top of that, this gap results in decreases in employee productivity, efficiency, and innovativeness.

This insight is the seed that bore the fruit of this book. Its mission is to try to close this gap, which it does by describing proven, clear, structured, and practical approaches for developing the digital workplace based on its mission and vision.

2.3   A NEW APPROACH IS REQUIRED

The word "technology" is related to the Greek word *téchnē*, which means "art", "craft", or "craftsmanship". Technology is intended to reduce the physical or mental load on us, and in general, raise our standard of living. However, the digital work environment in many organizations does the exact opposite of this. Therefore, we need to find our way back to this original meaning of technology. We need to put the people working in the digital work environment front and center. If we do this, then it will lead to the following results, among others:

- Fewer, easier to use, and more appealingly designed systems stripped of everything unnecessary.
- More consistently designed systems to ensure we feel at home with them and don't have to learn a whole new way of doing the same thing in different systems.
- Increased flexibility to do our work when and where we need to and in the way that suits us best.
- Better integration and seamless flow between systems so they follow the employees' workflows.
- Better performance and stability so we can always count on having what we need when we need it.

These may seem difficult to achieve for many organizations yet must be considered merely hygiene factors. The real challenge – and opportunity – of the digital workplace is utilizing new digital technology to find a smarter way to work together as an organization internally, as well as with customers or citizens, suppliers, partners, and others to add maximum value. This is where we find great opportunities in areas such as mobility, social collaboration, and in particular, artificial intelligence, which can connect employees when used correctly and amplify their individual and shared capabilities. If the hygiene factors are not in place, how will the organization be able to seize these opportunities?

2.4   AN EXAMPLE FOR INSPIRATION

Many municipalities and government agencies around the world will almost certainly have taken a close look at GOV.UK, a website which has received much attention for providing UK citizens with a single point of access to government services. This interest in GOV.UK is mainly based on how the public sector can offer more effective and uniform services to citizens. However, the same approach could be applied to a corporate group or other business as a way to host services for their employees in one place.

GOV.UK was developed by the Government Digital Service (GDS), a government organization that looks more like a startup. GDS was highly successful in employing a step-by-step approach to developing GOV.UK with a clear vision, and many municipalities around the world have tried to copy their recipe for success. They did this by copying or at least taking much inspiration from the design of GOV.UK when redesigning their own websites. But unfortunately, they missed the whole point of GOV.UK. The big secret of GOV.UK and the success of the website (which is not really a secret at all because GDS openly shares how the website is developed) lies in the approach taken by GDS – its *how*.

Their approach is characterized by a distinct *service-dominant logic*. Development is guided by well-expressed and modern *design principles*. For example, the organization starts with user needs instead of its own, bases decisions on empirical data, and focuses on simplicity, iterating over and over again to quickly learn what works more or less well. If there's anything that municipalities and government agencies should copy, it's the principles and ways of working employed by GDS. The key to success in improving the digital work environment lies in what approaches the organization takes in developing it. That's why, in this book, we present a structured, iterative, and user-centric approach to developing the digital workplace, from strategy to design. As with GDS, our approach is based on several guiding principles.

2.5 SIX GUIDING PRINCIPLES

The principles that form the basis for the approach we present in this book are user-centered, holistic, co-creative, evidencing, a value focus, and an iterative way of working (Figure 13).

| VALUE FOCUS | USER-CENTERED | HOLISTIC | ITERATIVE | CO-CREATIVE | EVIDENCING |

Figure 13. Guiding principles for development of the digital workplace.

Let's briefly go over these principles and how they are relevant to the development of the digital workplace.

2.5.1 VALUE FOCUS

> *If we can fall in love with serving people, creating value, solving problems, building valuable connections and doing work that matters, it makes it far more likely we're going to do important work.*[2]

– Seth Godin, entrepreneur and author

The value of a product or service is created when it is used. This applies to physical products and services as well as to IT systems and digital services. With this view, information technology is a means for creating value and not necessarily an end in itself. The focus of all IT development must therefore be on creating value. We do this by developing IT systems that solve the right problems in the right way and ensure that the employees know how best to use them.

---

2   Seth Godin, "Turning passion on its head, Seth´s blog (blog), August 30, 2014, https://seths.blog/2014/08/turning-passion-on-its-head/.

Focusing on value also involves avoiding and minimizing waste, in other words, anything that does not contribute to value creation. We should always try to eliminate the costs incurred as a result of unnecessary complexity and friction between a user and the services he or she uses by reducing precisely that complexity and friction.

2.5.2   USER-CENTERED

We spend a lot time designing the bridge, but not enough time thinking about the people who are crossing it.

– Dr Prabhjot Singh, Director of the Arnhold Institute for Global Health

To define what value is, we need to identify and understand who the users are, what they require, and what obstacles they face. We must always put the user front and center to maximize value creation and avoid waste. One way to do this is to always try to see everything through the lens of the user. Many of the problems found in our digital work environments have emerged as a result of the lack of a user-centered design. Changes are made without attempting to see how they impact the individual user's work environment and are experienced by the user.

2.5.3   HOLISTIC

Always design a thing by considering it in its next larger context – a chair in a room, a room in a house, a house in an environment, an environment in a city plan.

– Eliel Saarinen, Finnish-American architect and industrial designer

Many of the problems we see in the digital work environment result from the lack of a holistic view. Decisions are made to change individual parts without seeing how they will impact the whole, especially the users' work situation. If changing one part makes the users' work situation more difficult, this will make it harder for them to do their jobs, and they will create less value. Therefore, we must strive to see the whole and take the entire usage environment into consideration when changing the digital work environment, such as when designing a digital service. This also includes the physical work environment.

2.5.4   ITERATIVE

Control is for beginners. Iteration is truly the mother of invention.

– Deborah Mills-Scofield, innovation and strategy author

We can deal with uncertainty, complexity, and risks by taking many small steps instead of a couple large ones. We analyze every step we take to check how it's going, draw conclusions, and learn lessons about what does and does not work. Then, we adapt how we take the next steps. This enables us to quickly identify and manage risks before they are realized or cause too much damage and to change course if we end up on the wrong track. An iterative way of working also allows us to quickly produce and demonstrate results. In addition to making our progress clear to everyone, this allows us to put the results in the hands of the users and gain valuable feedback far before we are completely finished developing the solution.

2.5.5   CO-CREATIVE

Where do new ideas come from? The answer is simple: differences. Creativity comes from unlikely juxtapositions.

– Nicholas Negroponte, Greek-American architect and founder of MIT Media Lab

Another way to manage uncertainty and complexity besides using an iterative approach is to create multidisciplinary teams. This involves gathering all the skills and perspectives we might conceivably need to shed light on and understand a problem from all angles in order to determine what solutions are possible.

Co-creation is highly effective for developing something as complex as the digital workplace. We can involve all significant stakeholders as prospective users as well as any others who will be directly or indirectly affected by the planned change. This enables us to gain access to their ideas and perspectives, obtain information about their needs and circumstances, and most importantly, prepare to implement the change.

2.5.6   EVIDENCING

Nothing ever becomes real till it is experienced.

– John Keats, English poet

Information technology is abstract, especially before there is a finished product or service with which to interact. We need to use all the means at our disposal to transform our hypotheses, ideas, and solutions into tangible evidence if we are to understand the problem we seek to solve and find the best way to shape the solutions before we have a finished product or service. We employ a variety of methods to visualize and make that which is abstract more tangible, enabling us to gain an understanding early on of how a solution may look and function, and possibly even interact with it.

Evidencing is a principle applicable not only in service development but also in strategy development, where various visualization methods are employed to define the current ("as is") state, the future ("to be") state, and make the organization's plans more tangible and easier to adopt. We will often refer back to this and other principles in the following chapters, where we discuss them and show how they can be applied in both strategy development and in the design of the digital workplace.

2.6   SUMMARY

In this chapter we covered:

- How we define the digital workplace – a *digital work environment designed purposefully and holistically with the user front and center.*
- How it is important to first establish the purpose and the process before starting to work on the "what", and how the process is the key to creating a digital workplace that empowers people.
- What principles should guide the approach: value focus, user-centered, holistic, iterative, co-creative, and evidencing.

Now, we'll continue by outlining the foundation of our approach – service-dominant logic.

CHAPTER 3

SHIFTING FOCUS TO VALUE CREATION

3.1   INTRODUCTION

In many organizations, the employees struggle with systems that are difficult to use and an increasingly complex digital work environment. It is needlessly difficult for the employees to perform their tasks, and they frequently suffer from stress, unnecessary cognitive loads, and illness. For the organization, this translates into a decrease in efficiency, productivity, and innovativeness.

One significant cause of this situation is that no one will have realized or acted on the insight that an IT investment only adds value once used, thus enabling better, faster, and less resource-demanding ways of performing tasks. This insight is key in service-dominant logic.

A service is an action that provides utility, or value, to someone once delivered by satisfying their needs and expectations. Some classic examples include cleaning and babysitting or services provided during travel and hotel stays. However, the work that an application performs on your computer or via the cloud can also be considered a service. For example, sending an email using an email client is an action you perform with the help of the software, and this is a type of service (Figure 14).

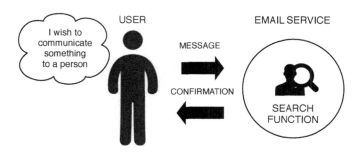

Figure 14. Email is a service that is rendered when the user uses an email client.

Service-dominant logic differs from the more traditional view of value creation, which is called goods-dominant logic. According to *goods-dominant logic*, value is created when a product is transferred from supplier to customer, in other words, when someone buys the product. In contrast, according to *service-dominant logic*, value is only created once the service is used.

The use of a service is inseparable from the rendering of a service. Although email clients give you the ability to write and send email, value is only created when you actually use the client. Therefore, the moment you write and send email is when the service is produced. This line of reasoning may be considered a little overly theoretical, yet it is highly important because it helps us understand when value is created – the moment a service is used.

Service-dominant logic also considers how resources are created, organized, reused, and made available in the form of services. This opens up more flexible and effective ways of providing resources. We explain this in greater detail at the end of the chapter.

Finally, service-dominant logic can be linked to a strong overall trend in our society and economy – servicification.

3.2   SERVICIFICATION – A STRONG TREND

The economies of the developed world are experiencing an ongoing shift from the production of products to the production of services. According to the World Bank, the service economy currently makes up three-fourths of the economy in the wealthier regions of the world and approximately half of the economy in the less wealthy areas. The trend is clear. Service production's share of the economy increased by four percent in the wealthier regions of the world between 2000–2014 alone, which means that the production of goods decreased by the same percentage.[34] This may not sound like a lot, but it refers to the total world production, and the time frame has been relatively short.

---

34   *World Development Indicators: Structure of output* (The World Bank, 2016), http://wdi.worldbank.org/table/4.2.

The trend becomes even more striking when viewed from a longer perspective, and the US serves as a good example (Figure 15).

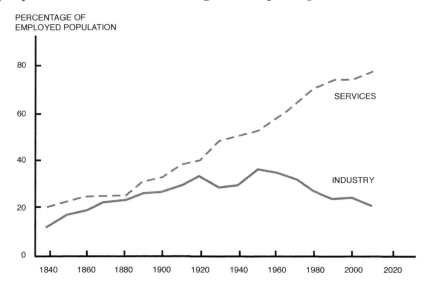

Figure 15. Percentage of US workforce employed in the services and industry sectors.[35]

Fifty years ago, a little more than half the US working population was employed in the service sector. Today, this figure is approximately 80 percent. This trend is not only driven by factors such as automation and decreased dependence on human labor in agriculture and the industrial sector but also is the result of a more profound change taking place in our values and behaviors as consumers. The more our material wealth increases, the more important immaterial values and experiences become for people in the developed world. At the same time, there is an increasing trend toward the conservation of existing resources for the sake of both the economy and environment. New technology opens up new possibilities for servicification and resource conservation, for example, through sharing platforms such as AirBnB, thus reinforcing the trend.

35   Louis D. Johnston, *History lessons: Understanding the decline in manufacturing* (Minnpost, 2012).

With ownership comes great responsibility. If something breaks or stops working, we have to take care of it and pay for it ourselves, such as in the case of a vacation property. Why should we spend a lot of money on the property and assume these risks when, instead, we could pay only for the time we actually use and benefit from it? By purchasing services, we avoid the responsibility and risk associated with purchasing a product. This allows us to stay fully focused on obtaining the value and experience we seek. More and more people, especially the younger generations, are beginning to think this way. For them and a growing number of others, ownership is no longer an end in itself.

Servicification means that products are increasingly seen as platforms for delivering services. For example, in the future, instead of buying a car, we will buy transportation when we need it. We know what we are getting, avoid a bunch of risks and hassle such as maintenance, and get a price that is transparent and predictable. There are no hidden costs for repairs and maintenance that we suddenly find we have to cover.

Once self-driving cars fully take off among mainstream consumers, our behavior will change, not only in the automotive and transportation industries but also in the way our communities look and function. Why would we need so many parking spaces in our cities when we could travel in self-driving cars moving people and goods around the clock? And how many cars will we need anyway if we all share the existing capacity?

The extensive and rapid servicification of the economy is occurring at the same time as – and largely as a result of – the increasing rate of digitalization. In the digital world, which uses the internet as a distribution platform, new services can be continuously invented and provided, especially with sharing platforms such as AirBnB, where ordinary people can rent their property to those who wish to use it. At the same time, this upends existing laws and regulations, which must eventually be adapted to the new behaviors we develop as consumers.

The individual or organization that provides the service (the service provider) charges for use of the service instead of for transferring ownership of a physical product to the customer. To ensure a viable business, the service provider must ideally persuade us to want to purchase the service over and over again and preferably start a subscription or sign a long-term contract. But this will not happen unless we are satisfied with the service – otherwise, we could leave as quickly as we came. Our expectations must be met and preferably exceeded time and time again. Thus, it is crucial for a service provider to understand the needs and expectations of its customers and users as much as possible.

For product vendors, sometimes developing a product that we find sufficiently appealing and good value for money is enough to make us want to buy it. However, we might only buy it once. We may not realize that this was not in fact such a good investment for quite some time because we do not use or directly benefit from the product as much as we thought we would. Or maybe we will try to sell it on to someone else.

Here, digitalization is also playing an increasingly larger role by matching the products we do not use with those who might want them and may be willing to pay us for them. For many years, goods-dominant logic has dominated our view of IT system implementation. Our primary focus has been on purchasing and operating hardware and software in addition to developing various IT solutions. Far too little focus has been dedicated to defining and ensuring the intended value and experiences of using these. The job is usually considered done once the IT system is fully developed and installed, but that should be only the beginning of the work to create value.

3.3   GETTING THE BASICS RIGHT

Given that service-dominant logic plays such a key role in both digitalization and the development of the digital workplace, we need to explain a couple basic terms before we move on. We will start with the most important one in the context of the digital workplace – digital service.

3.3.1   DIGITAL SERVICES

A *service* is an action that creates value for someone by meeting one or more of their needs. If we order window cleaning, our need is for the windows to be clean, and value is what we get when we look out through the clean glass. A *digital service* is a service that uses digital hardware and software, which is increasingly provided over the internet; for example, a search service to find information on the internet such as Google or Bing, or a service to store and share documents and other files such as Dropbox or Box.

Digital services differ greatly from physical services. The biggest difference is that the provision of a digital service is fully automatic. No human involvement is required to deliver the service to me. As a user, I am also in full control of when I want to use it. It is there when I need it.

As an employee, I use digital services to perform a variety of tasks, such as holding an online meeting, preparing a presentation, or filling out a timesheet. I can also use them to read up on something or take an online course. But how does a digital service work? Let's explain with an example (Figure 16).

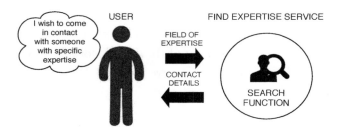

Figure 16. Example of a digital service.

Let's say that you need to find and contact a colleague with specific expertise, such as survey design. You don't yet know if any of your colleagues have this expertise and, if so, who? The service you decide to use is a search function that enables you to find people based on various fields of expertise. When you search, the search function finds those colleagues that have stated they have the expertise in question. It gives details that include a photo, name, and contact information of the colleagues that match your search criteria.

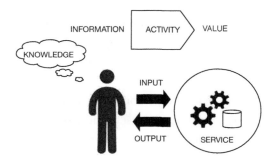

Figure 17. Knowledge workers use refined information to create value.

Figure 17 illustrates, in principle, how a digital service helps the user create value. The user gives the service information and receives information in return that can be used to perform an activity that creates value when combined with the user's prior knowledge.

3.3.2   CUSTOMERS AND USERS

Two terms that can sometimes be confusing when talking about services are "customer" and "user". Therefore, let's see how they relate to one another (Figure 18).

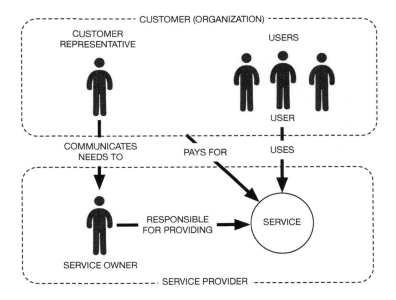

Figure 18. Relationship between customer, user, and service provider.

A *customer* pays for a service and is normally seen as the one who seeks the value of the service. The *user* is the one who uses a service. One individual could serve as both customer and user, but this is not always the case – especially for organizations, where the customer is often a legal entity (the organization), while the users are a group of or all the employees within the organization. The organization pays for several digital services it wants its employees to use in their work, making it the customer of another organization, the *service provider*. Before paying for a new service, the customer communicates what is needed to the service provider in a suitable manner to ensure that the service can meet these needs. The person responsible for the development and delivery of a service within the service provider's organization is usually called the *service owner*.

3.3.3   VALUE

For physical services, the value of a service is created the moment it is used. An example of this is how, when a window is being cleaned, it simultaneously becomes cleaned. However, because the results of using digital services are often in the form of information, if we follow our previous reasoning, then value might not be created until long after the services are used – or maybe not even at all. It simply depends on whether the information proves useful (Figure 19).

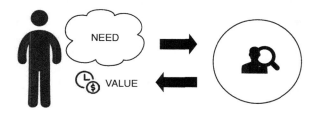

Figure 19. Value is not created until the user's need is met.

Whether or not value is created, and further, how it is created is a subjective matter and determined mainly by the user or customer. Therefore, it is absolutely crucial that service providers gain an understanding of the user, their tasks and goals, and what situations they need the service for.

3.3.4   USER EXPERIENCE

If you find an employee with the expertise you're looking for, but the process was frustrating because of the messy way the search results were displayed, then this will likely have a negative impact on how you experience the value. This is why it is important that the service creates a positive user experience. ISO 9241-210 defines *user experience* as:

> *"A person's perceptions and responses that result from the use or anticipated use of a product, system or service."*[36]

---

36   *Ergonomics of human-system interaction - Part 210: Human-centred design for interactive systems* (ISO 9241-210:2010, 2015), https://www.iso.org/standard/52075.html.

All users have an experience when using services, good or bad. If the user experience is positive, the value of using the service will likely be considered greater than a negative experience would give. Therefore, the user experience must be as positive as possible for us to get the maximum value out of a digital service.

Most of the services we use at work are utility-centric; in other words, they help us perform our tasks in order to create business value. In other contexts, we may want to relax, find inspiration, escape from reality, waste time, or connect with other people instead. We can thus differentiate between utility-centric and entertainment-centric digital services. The latter include various types of games, video streaming services, and music services. Entertainment-centric services can also be physical, such as vacations, spa treatments, and movies.

Although most of the digital services we use at work are utility-centric, we simply cannot afford to ignore the entertainment aspects of a user experience. For example, if a time-reporting service is difficult to use, we may postpone reporting our time, which could delay invoicing. We also end up having to spend too much unnecessary time on a task that does not create any value per se. The user experience may also cause frustration and stress in a way that saps our motivation and ability to perform well at work. If we can design the user experience to be more entertaining, even mundane tasks might become fun to do.

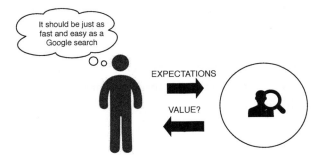

Figure 20. Our expectations and behaviors influence our experience of value.

In addition, the expectations we have prior to using a service play a key role in our user experience, as illustrated in Figure 20. Our expectations set the bar the service must reach and preferably exceed. What the service provider has promised us, what we have previously seen and heard about the service, and our experiences from using similar services are among the factors that determine where this bar is set.

Our growing experience using digital services as individuals is increasingly informing what we expect of our digital workplace and the services we are expected to use at work. For example, many people compare internal search functions with Google's search function, and they wish their search function was as fast and easy and their results as well displayed and easy to navigate as Google's.

3.3.5   PRODUCTS

Where do we draw the line between what a product is and what a service is? This question is frequently raised when talking about goods and services, and it's not easy to draw a clear line. In service-dominant logic, it's a little bit easier: a product is simply a mechanism for delivering one or more services.

Take an ATM, for example. An ATM is a product purchased by a bank and installed at a public place or a bank branch. It is then used to deliver services, such as cash withdrawals and account balance information, to the bank's customers. If these services cannot be rendered, the ATM is useless for both the service provider (the bank) and the user (the bank customer). At the same time, the product's characteristics and design play a crucial role in the user experience and perceived value. Hasn't everyone at some point cursed at an ATM for its design or for taking too long to complete a cash withdrawal?

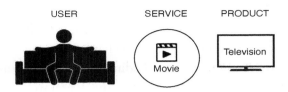

USER   SERVICE   PRODUCT

Figure 21. A product is a mechanism for delivering services.

An example most of us can relate to is that of televisions for watching TV (Figure 21). If you buy a television, you are buying a product. You want to use the product to watch TV, movies, and video streaming services, or maybe play video games. You won't get any value out of it until you use it for one of these purposes. This is also the point when you'll know whether the product meets your expectations in terms of aspects such as image and sound quality. Thus, the television is a mechanism for delivering services.

3.3.6   CHANNELS

Some services are provided both digitally and physically. For example, as a bank customer, you can check your bank account balance via online banking or a mobile app, but you can also visit a physical bank branch to inquire about your account balance. The service is essentially the same even though the user experience may differ significantly.

When we talk about the digital workplace, we refer to digital services delivered via digital channels. Various digital channels, such as the internet, email, and social media, are most relevant to discuss in the context of communication and interaction between organizations and customers. For the digital workplace, the concept of channels is not as important. Instead, we talk about digital services being made available across various devices.

However, when planning and designing digital services and the digital workplace, we should bear in mind that services in the digital workplace must sometimes be delivered via physical channels as well. We need to try to see the big picture instead of dividing the world into digital and physical as if they are unrelated opposites. The digital workplace must be seamlessly integrated with the physical workplace.

For example, if you need a new password for your user account, you may be able to send a request through a website, mobile app, or email – digital channels that all fall within the scope of the digital workplace. But if you cannot log in to your computer because you have forgotten your password, then it actually makes sense that you can also reach this service via your phone. The owner of the "new password" service should therefore be responsible for delivering it not only in digital channels but also in physical channels. From this perspective, the digital workplace is simply an environment for delivering an equivalent service digitally.

3.3.7   DEVICES

The user interacts with digital services via a type of device, such as a computer, tablet, or smartphone (Figure 22).

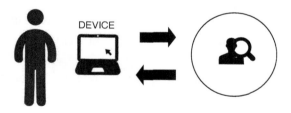

Figure 22. We interact with services via various devices.

In digital marketing, services such as the internet, mobile apps, social media, email, and text messages are often held up as examples of digital channels. This division is, in fact, of no particular interest to the user.

In reality, it is sometimes difficult to differentiate between them; for example, mobile apps increasingly consist of mobile-friendly versions of websites, and many chat services strive to avoid differences between messages sent as text messages and those sent over the internet via mobile apps or websites. In this context, it is more important to understand what types of devices there are and what tasks and usage situations each device is best suited for, as they each have specific capabilities and limitations. Figure 23 shows some of the devices that may be found at a workplace.

Figure 23. Types of devices typically found in a workplace.

As users, we often choose the device or devices we think are best suited to our current situation. For a positive user experience, a digital service must be easy for us to use via the device best suited to our current situation. Our personal preferences also play a role in what device we choose. Let's take an example (Figure 24). Say that you are communicating with a colleague via chat while sitting in front of your computer in the office. Later in the day while riding the bus home, your colleague sends a new message and brings up the conversation again. Your smartwatch alerts you to the new message, which is easy to respond to with just a few taps on the watch. The response you receive is a message that requires a longer answer, so you pick up your phone to continue the conversation.

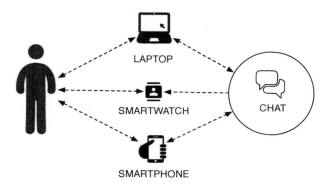

Figure 24. The same service can be used across multiple devices.

It's easier to understand what type of device is best suited for a specific activity and usage situation if we categorize each device available. We can do this by asking and answering certain questions:

- Is it designed for mobile or stationary use?
- Is it designed for individual or group use?
- Who owns and controls it? The individual or the organization?
- Is it mainly used for consumption or production?
- In what type of environment will it be used (sound, light, humidity)?

As an example, take a group of employees monitoring traffic in a mobile network from a surveillance room. The devices do not need to be mobile because the work is carried out in a specific location. They are owned and controlled by the company because the information being processed is sensitive in nature. A shared video wall is used to display the information everyone in the room should monitor. The wall is used solely for presenting information, in other words, consumption. When employees need information to perform their individual tasks, they use the desktop computers at their workstations. These are used for both consumption and production.

3.3.8   USAGE SITUATIONS

We have already touched on the term "usage situation", but further explanation may be required, as it plays a key role in designing the digital workplace and digital services.

A *situation* can be described as all the circumstances affecting one or more employees when they are to perform an activity at a specific place and time. In addition, when an employee needs to use one or more digital services in a specific situation, this is what we call a *usage situation* (Figure 25).

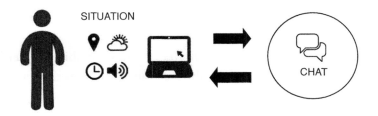

Figure 25. The usage situation is when and where the service is used.

Of course, usage situations can differ significantly depending on the type of business and the position and tasks of the employee. Typical knowledge workers such as engineers, programmers, managers, journalists, and architects may need digital services not only at their desk but also in a client's meeting room, a café in town, at their kitchen table, while walking somewhere, or when traveling by air or rail.

However, today, people in professions that are not traditionally rooted in office work – such as doctors and healthcare staff, teachers, service technicians, flight attendants, retail staff, and factory workers – need access to digital services in their day-to-day work. Their usage situations often have unique conditions and limitations.

In Figure 26, we illustrate some usage situations of employees depending on what type of work they do.

IN A MEETING ROOM	TRAVELING	WALKING	AT A CONSTRUCTION SITE
IN A FACTORY	AT AN OFFICE DESK	AT A CAFÉ	IN A TREATMENT ROOM

Figure 26. Examples of usage situations.

The situations we find ourselves in inevitably affect our ability to perform our tasks. Sometimes this involves the location, sometimes the time, sometimes the environment. It's often a combination of conditions, limitations, and events associated with both the time and place. Depending on the type of usage situation, we also tend to enter one of these three work modes when performing a certain type of task:

- Focused productivity
- Urgent action
- Passive consumption

The simplest definition of a *work mode* is a classification of tasks that can help us decide what type of device is best suited for performing a specific task.

The usage situation plays a major role not only in our choice of device but also in what we should be able to do with the service and how it should be designed. Different devices, surroundings, and ways to connect to the internet are just a few factors that impact how a digital service must be designed to make it usable and safe in the relevant usage situation.

To choose the right digital services and find the best way to design them, we must start by building an understanding of the users, what work they need to do, and most importantly, what usage situations they will be in when they need to use the services.

3.3.9   USAGE PATTERNS

Using digital services in our personal lives causes us to change our existing behavior or develop new behaviors. Digital technology gives us new capabilities and thus new behaviors, such as sharing video from a smartphone to another screen or choosing to find something based on your current location. This in turn influences what we expect from the digital services we use at work.

Changing our behavior is difficult. "Reprogramming" ourselves and our habitual behaviors requires a big effort. If the change is for the better, as in it makes performing a specific task easier with fewer steps, then we might think it's worth the effort. But what if the change is for the worse? Then forget about it! Once we've experienced how easy and comfortable something can be, like when we find a shortcut, we don't want to give that up. The moment we find ourselves in the same or a similar situation, we expect to be able to take that shortcut. Digitalization creates new shortcuts all the time – we call them *usage patterns*. Figure 27 illustrates some examples of usage patterns.

Figure 27. Examples of usage patterns.

To make what we mean by "usage pattern" clearer, we have created an outline of this using one or more digital services in the following table.

Usage pattern	Examples in practice
Motivate me Motivates me to do something.	**Supermarket wellness discount app** I get a 0.5% discount for every kilometer I walk or run.
Reward me Rewards me when I have achieved something.	**Supermarket wellness discount app** I get a new discount when I have taken 10,000 steps.
Recognize my achievements Acknowledges when I have done a good job at something.	**Runkeeper** Congratulates me on completing a run.
Remind me Reminds me of an event or activity at a certain time and/or place.	**Google Calendar** I am reminded that my meeting starts in 10 minutes.
Make me aware Makes me aware of useful information.	**Waze** I learn that the southbound lanes of a nearby highway are closed from the next exit due to an accident.
Notify me Notifies me of something I need to act on.	**Parkster** I am notified that my parking expires in 30 minutes.
Use my position Gives me suggestions or reminders based on my location.	**Uber** I can see which cars are available near my position or another position.
Save for later Saves something to be used later.	**Netflix** I can add a film to my favorites so I can watch it later.
Predict my next step Predicts what I most likely want to do next and asks me about it.	**Norwegian** I am asked if I want to book a hotel after booking a flight.

It is important to recognize and understand various usage patterns when designing digital services, as this enables us to create a service that is experienced as easy and convenient.

3.4   DESIGNING A SEAMLESS WORKPLACE

As implied in our reasoning on usage situations, it is important to consider the physical work environment when shaping the digital workplace and its services. This is precisely where many organizations fall short. The physical and digital work environments are often treated like two planets that rarely cross orbits. As a result, they are poorly integrated and make it more difficult for employees to do their jobs. Take the conference room, for example, where connecting any device to a screen and sharing what you see with others participating via a web meeting service is anything but fast and painless.

Again, the cause is usually organizational in nature. Responsibility for the physical workplace and for the digital workplace is often siloed in different parts of the organization that are managed by people with completely different assignments, skills, and points of view. Rarely, if ever, do they engage in structured or close coordination. Integration is particularly important in places where the organization has control and can influence the design of both the digital and physical workplace, such as an office, a store, a classroom, or a clinic.

3.4.1   SUPPORT THE USER JOURNEY

The use of a digital service can be viewed through two primary lenses: that of the user and that of the service provider. The service delivery process specifies the intended user interaction with the service, and the usage process is how the user uses the service in practice to achieve a result – the actual outcome – but the exact details of this are impossible to predict.

Each point of interaction with a service is called a *touchpoint*. In the physical world, the touchpoint could be a phone call with a person from the service provider, a physical location, a machine, some form of printed material, or an object. In the digital world, touchpoints consist of a device such as a computer or smartphone and the user interface of a digital service.

The touchpoints of a service can occur in an almost infinite variety of usage processes. Rarely is any usage process the same as another for reasons such as different conditions and limitations in the usage environment, different goals, and different user preferences and behaviors.

Therefore, to find the best way to design a service and its touchpoints, we must attempt to understand the most common usage processes. Having only one variation rarely works, but supporting too many variations of usage processes is not usually financially sustainable. A good way to build understanding of a usage process is to create a *user journey* – a visual representation of a user's interactions with a service to achieve a specific goal. Using a term that indicates which stakeholder is involved, such as "customer journey" or "employee journey", is often more specific than the more general term, "user journey".

The interface between physical and digital work environments consists of the various devices we use to access digital services, in other words, the devices we bring with us which are often personal, such as smartphones and computers, as well as the shared devices of the space, such as videoconferencing equipment or the controls for shades, lighting, or audio in a room. We can regard these devices as portals between the physical and digital worlds that facilitate integration and interaction.

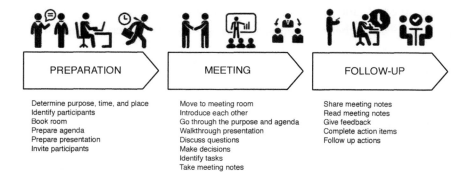

Figure 28. Meeting process from preparation to follow-up.

Perhaps the most telling example of what can happen in the case of deficient integration between the physical workplace and the digital workplace is with meetings (Figure 28). Few meetings nowadays are strictly analog with a paper, pen, and whiteboard. Some form of digital tool is usually involved. You might need to show a presentation on a projector screen or TV, but it can be a challenge to connect your preferred device and get the presentation to display on the screen or TV. The lack of connectivity options, poor placement of cables and outlets, and incompatibility between devices can easily create problems that drain time and energy from the meeting. This translates into an enormous amount of wasted time and energy, especially as many organizations allow meetings to flood their employees' calendars.

Seamless integration is all the more important when the meeting involves remote participants via a web meeting service. More than anything, audio and visual communication must work in both directions.

Most web meeting services include a chat feature, document and screen sharing, and sometimes even a virtual whiteboard. However, those on site may want to use the physical equipment in the room, such as a whiteboard. The meeting will not be effective unless remote attendees can participate. At the very least, they must be able to see what is written on the whiteboard in the room. Preferably, they should also be able to create and share content. This naturally requires effective integration between the physical and digital work environments. Otherwise, both creativity and productivity will suffer at the many work meetings requiring remote participation.

If we look not only at the meeting but also the entire journey from the decision to hold the meeting to the time to follow up on the results, it's clear that many transitions between activities and usage situations are not always painless and seamless.

3.4.2   THE NATURE OF KNOWLEDGE WORK

It is only by understanding both the nature of the process and the potential usage situations of the employees that we can begin to improve integration and minimize friction.

The processes of knowledge work are usually difficult to predict. Employees themselves often do not know in advance what activities they will need to perform or in what order. To quote a former colleague, "I do not follow a process but rather select from a cloud of activities." This means he chooses the activities he needs from this bundle and then does them in the most suitable order (Figure 29).

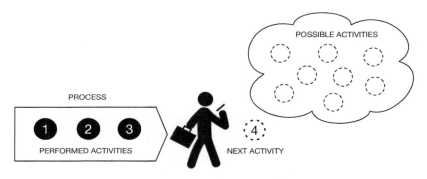

Figure 29. The knowledge worker selects from a "cloud of activities".

Employees thus shape their own process (Figure 30). One or more IT systems are often used to perform these activities, which may need to be performed in different situations such as at a desk, in a meeting room, or on the go.

Figure 30. Example of a knowledge worker's process,

In other words, both flexibility and support are required to allow employees to easily shape their own process. This requires that the digital services are available and tailored to the relevant usage situations. The work can only go as smoothly as possible if the digital services used interoperate and make it easy to move from one activity to the next and from one usage situation to another.

3.4.3   CONSIDER THE ECOSYSTEM OF SERVICES

Unfortunately, this is precisely what the digital work environment utterly fails to do in many organizations. People in various domains have purchased and implemented a variety of systems and tools aimed at streamlining individual activities and processes. However, this has almost always been done without considering how these fit into the bigger picture.

In addition, the functionality employees need in order to perform various activities is often locked into monolithic systems designed to be used individually, not in conjunction with other systems. These systems often look and behave in different ways and include overlapping functionalities, and most of all, are not designed for the situations when employees need to use them – having to log into several different systems can suck the life out of anyone.

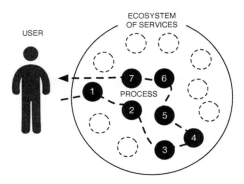

Figure 31. Services exist and are used in an ecosystem of services.

A holistic view of the role a digital service plays in the ecosystem is essential when choosing and designing a digital service. Employees must be able to navigate their way forward conveniently in line with the way they need to work, which is illustrated in Figure 31.

3.5   SERVICE ORIENTATION

"Service orientation" is a term closely associated with servicification, and they can be seen as two sides of the same coin. Servicification is about what service providers offer customers and users and how value is created, while *service orientation* is about how the service provider produces and packages this offering.

The simplest explanation of service orientation is that an IT system (or a business) is divided into a number of components whereby each performs an autonomous task. These components thus render a service and are considered services. The services can then be composed in new ways to meet new customer needs or to be offered to other businesses.

For example, Amazon's e-commerce platform is based on a service-oriented architecture. In addition to using this for its internet retail store, in 2006, Amazon started offering services that allow others to build and host websites and applications through its subsidiary, Amazon Web Services. Now Amazon offers more than 70 services used by over one million customers including big names such as Pinterest, Netflix, and NASA.

Service orientation has its roots in a system development principle called *separation of concerns*, which is based on the idea that you break down large problems into subproblems to make them easier to solve. For example, the same principle can be applied when breaking down a business process into smaller components in order to localize specific events in the process. These can then be defined as services that can be reused, composed, customized, and provided to satisfy the various needs of one or more customers.

Service-oriented architecture is a style of architecture for creating, providing, and using services. This concept not only affects the digital work environment but also changes the entire business eventually. In light of this, service-oriented architecture should not be treated merely as a technical concept relegated to technical specialists at the IT department.

There is much to gain from service orientation and service-oriented architecture, such as lower costs and higher quality through reuse. They also make it possible to create new services or processes faster to meet new or changed demands. However, the truly significant value of service orientation is that it helps suppliers achieve a change from an inside-out to an outside-in perspective.

Successful service orientation requires a profound understanding of what customers and users need and what they consider a service. It takes walking in their shoes to find out what they need to be able to do, what situations they often find themselves in, and what experiences they have when using a service. Making guesses and assumptions from inside our silo or asking the supplier can quickly turn counterproductive. And yet, many IT projects are conducted this way, especially in the case of IT systems for employees.

Thomas Erl defines eight principles for understanding how we should view digital services.[37] Here, we have selected the four that are the most important: service discoverability, service abstraction, service composability, and loose coupling.

---

37 Thomas Erl, *Service-Oriented Architecture: Concepts, Technology, and Design* (Prentice Hall, 2005).

3.4.1   SERVICE DISCOVERABILITY

When you go to find a book in the library, it first needs to have been described in some way and preferably included in a searchable registry. This is also the case if digital services are to be discoverable and usable by other services or users. The service catalog is this type of registry, and it should contain information about the services (metadata) that makes them easy to find.

Much effort is put into making consumer-centric digital services discoverable, but nothing close to this effort is made for internal services. More often than not, the offering and where to find the services is unclear: *How can I find what I need? Is this something for me?* Think about how, when you walk into McDonald's, you don't have to search long before you find the menu.

3.4.2   SERVICE ABSTRACTION

Simply put, the *principle of abstraction* means that, as users, we shouldn't have to care about who produces services, with what methods, and how. The only part of a service that should be visible to us is its interface.

As users, we are interested in the value we hope to get out of using the service. We also want the user experience to be as simple and convenient as possible. Therefore, if the service provider can conceal as much of the complexity as possible, then we can avoid the things that we consider irrelevant. For example, if we use a service like Dropbox to share documents and files with others, we don't need to know which servers the documents are stored on or what programming language was used to develop the service. As users, the less we need to know about how the service is delivered, the better.

3.4.3   SERVICE COMPOSABILITY

One service can be composed of several other services. The composition of two or more services can provide greater utility and value for customers or users than when used individually.

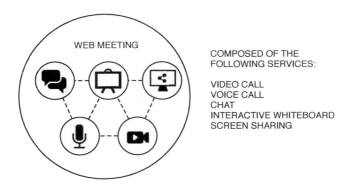

Figure 32. A web meeting service may be composed of several other services.

For example, let's consider a web meeting service (Figure 32). It is normally composed of several other services that can be delivered and used individually, such as video calling, voice calling, chatting, virtual whiteboarding, and screen sharing. Instead of being divided into separate services that the participants use individually, they are composed into one consistently designed service that makes it fast and easy to switch between each function.

3.4.4   LOOSE COUPLING

Services are designed for integration with each other without being dependent on one another. If we take the web meeting service as an example, this includes services such as voice calling and video calling. Although voice and video calling can be combined and used together seamlessly, they are independent of one another and can also be used individually.

3.6   AN EXAMPLE OF SERVICE ORIENTATION

Service orientation must always start with the mission, goals, and challenges of the business. Many initiatives in service orientation and service-oriented architecture have been overly focused on technical implementation. This is another reason why many initiatives fail to create business value.

Let's use an example from McDonald's to demonstrate how service orientation can create business value through a clear business focus.

Around a decade ago, McDonald's set out to improve drive-thru order taking at over 40 restaurants in the Los Angeles area because the restaurant staff often got customer orders wrong.[38] Many orders had to be redone and the incorrectly ordered food was thrown out. Considering that drive-thru sales in the US accounted for more than 70 percent of total McDonald's sales, this was naturally a serious problem with a negative impact on profitability.

The main reason for incorrect drive-thru orders was communication difficulties between the customer and the employee who took the order. For starters, the distance from the microphone combined with engine noise and other ambient noise made it difficult for both the customer and the order taker in the kitchen to hear everything being said. In addition, the kitchen, where the staff had to take orders and place them correctly in the order system, was often chaotic and stressful. On top of that, many local McDonald's employees were native Spanish speakers, which created a language barrier between the customer and the order taker. In other words, the situation was ripe for misunderstanding.

---

38 Matt Richter, "The Long-Distance Journey of a Fast-Food Order," *The New York Times*, April 11, 2006, https://www.nytimes.com/2006/04/11/technology/the-longdistance-journey-of-a-fastfood-order.html.

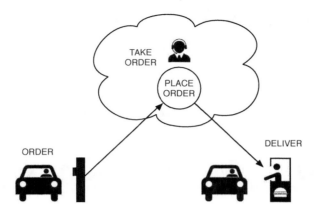

Figure 33. Service orientation of McDonald's drive-thru order taking.

McDonald's solution to this problem was as brilliant as it was simple (Figure 33). When placing an order, the customer was connected to a call center where native English-speaking staff took the order in a noise-free environment and entered it in the order system of the relevant restaurant. The call center was more than 200 kilometers away from Los Angeles, but in principle, it could very well have been located anywhere. The key to this solution was viewing order taking as a service. With the help of digital technology, people other than those who worked at the restaurant were able to provide the service.

In addition to better customer service and less waste, pure efficiency gains were also observed due to better use of resources, as the call center staff could take a large volume of orders from multiple McDonald's restaurants. In other words, the service could be (re)used by several restaurants with the cost shared among them.

The McDonald's drive-thru example illustrates how important it is to allow the business perspective to lead the way in the context of service orientation. Technology is an enabler, but the point of departure must be that you understand the business and its challenges along with the situation and needs of the users.

3.7   PUTTING IT ALL TOGETHER

We conclude this chapter by illustrating how everything is interrelated. Figure 34 shows how each part works together.

Figure 34. From usage situations to different types of information.

The figure reads from top to bottom. It starts with an employee using a service via a specific device in a specific usage situation. In order to give the user the desired value, the service delivers the information that meets the user's needs, which is done using the functionality of one or more digital platforms.

Let's take an example where, while riding the bus on the way to work, an employee uses a news app to read about their company. The touchpoint with the service is via a device, in this case, a smartphone. The news the employee reads is created and published with a digital platform, a publication platform. The information the employee then accesses is conveyed in the form of a web page with text and images. We have not previously addressed two of the aforementioned terms. One term, "information", surely does not need any further explanation. In this overview, the information is represented by various types of content that convey information, such as documents and web pages.

The other term not previously addressed is "digital platforms", and that does require an explanation, although we go on to describe it in more detail in chapter 4. When we say digital platforms, we are referring to a package of functionalities made by a supplier. These functionalities can then be used in one or more digital services.

To explain what a digital platform is, let's look at a digital platform currently used by more than one billion people – Facebook. Today, Facebook can be considered a digital platform. It has an ecosystem around it with countless digital services that use some of the functionality (and information) that Facebook offers. Spotify, Runkeeper, and Candy Crush are all examples of digital services that use Facebook's functionality to retrieve information about the Facebook users' social networks. For example, a Spotify user can see and share playlists with other Facebook friends who use Spotify. Similarly, a Runkeeper user can view, like, and comment on the activities Facebook friends track with Runkeeper, while Candy Crush players can see how well their Facebook friends are doing in the game. Even more services use Facebook's identity management functionality, which enables users to register and log in to their services with their Facebook identity.

These services have chosen to use certain types of functionality from a platform that offers it instead of developing their own. They choose this option because they not only avoid spending time and resources on development but also can take advantage of the information Facebook has about its users to improve their service. At the same time, Facebook naturally sees the advantage of this because it can collect more data about its users and thus offer advertisers even more accuracy for their ads.

3.8 SUMMARY

In this chapter we covered:

- What servicification is and why it is important to think in terms of services to maximize the value created from using digital services.
- How service-dominant logic can be applied to the development of the digital workplace and how key concepts are defined.
- How service orientation allows organizations to efficiently produce and provide digital services to their employees.

Now that we are starting to see the bigger picture, how do we go about achieving the desired change? We answer this in the next chapter.

CHAPTER 4

DEVELOPING A STRATEGY

4.1   INTRODUCTION

How do we quickly start developing our organization's digital workplace to empower the employees and boost the organization's productivity and innovativeness? How do we find a direction and set goals for the change required? And how do we identify what needs to be done, who should do it, and when it needs to be done in order to achieve this?

These are some of the crucial questions we answer as we describe how to create a digital workplace strategy.

4.1.1   STRATEGY IS ABOUT EXPLORING THE FUTURE

Strategy entails finding the direction you want to move in and then making smart decisions that enable you to get there. But in a complex and chaotic world, this is easier said than done. Given the dynamics and high rate of change driven by digital development, it's not possible to make an exact plan and then follow it precisely.

Therefore, a strategy is at best a guess of how we could and should navigate and position ourselves for success. The strategy must be continuously scrutinized and reworked to keep up with external changes.

So, do we even need a strategy at all? Yes, without a strategy, an organization is left coasting, clueless about what path to take when at a crossroads. This results in numerous ad hoc decisions made by various parts of the organization without a common direction and coordination, which results in unnecessary complexity, fragmentation, and suboptimization. In addition, no outdated services are phased out – everything is just added on top of the existing systems. This is why the digital work environment is often in such poor condition.

A (common) strategy allows us instead to make intelligent and well-founded assumptions about the best way for the organization to harness new opportunities and utilize its capabilities to achieve its goals.

We see *strategic thinking* as a way of exploring the future and a tool for challenging established ways of thinking and working. This should not be done only once or in five-year intervals but in an ongoing process. The strategy must be re-evaluated, adapted, and refined as conditions change and new options emerge.

Strategic thinking is particularly important in the digitalization of a business because it requires a sharp focus on experiences, content, and both fast and frequent changes. This also requires a greater degree of experimentation and risk-taking compared with traditional IT development.

If an organization aspires to provide a digital workplace that enables instead of limits the digitalization of its business, it must be responsive to and make the most of new digital opportunities. This necessitates that it be capable of actions such as:

- Continuously identifying and investigating digital opportunities and demonstrating how they can add value to the business.
- Understanding and acting on digital opportunities that can lead to completely new or significantly changed business models and customer experiences.

So, what is required to call something a strategy? And what characterizes an effective strategy?

4.1.2   CHARACTERISTICS OF AN EFFECTIVE STRATEGY

Some believe that a strategy describes a vision of the future, while others believe that it is a long-term plan of activities. In our view, a strategy must contain both a vision of the future and a long-term plan. But most of all, as already alluded to, strategy development is a process. The vision and long-term plan are snapshots of the strategy created during the strategy process.

A complete strategy consists of the following components:

- **The current state:** A description of the current situation – a specific and truthful view of where an organization stands today.
- **The future state:** A description of a desired future state, which clearly shows where the organization will be at a specific point in time. The future state is made tangible with several goals.
- **The vision:** A clear and engaging way of describing what the organization seeks to achieve in the long term.
- **The roadmap:** An overall plan showing, step by step, how an organization can bridge the gap between the current and future states to ultimately achieve its vision.

Figure 36 shows how all the parts of the strategy relate to each other. At the bottom, serving as the foundation of the strategy, we have the purpose of the business, or its mission, as we call it. This sets the playing field for the strategy.

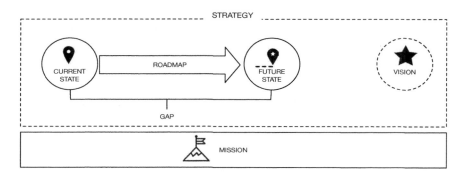

Figure 36. The components of a strategy.

Even if a strategy is complete, that is to say, it contains all the components above, many strategy documents end up on a shelf or in a document library gathering physical or digital dust. They are unused, and the strategies they contain are never realized. Why does this happen?

One common reason is the mistake of writing short, text-based documents that leave much room for interpretation, rendering decision-making on their basis difficult. Another is allowing strategy documents to be flooded with number-heavy statistics and complex diagrams, which rarely provide a tangible view of the desired future or what path must be taken to get there.

To avoid this, the strategy must be communicative and focused on results. It must meet four basic criteria:

- **Clear ownership:** If no one champions the strategy and is passionate about implementing it, then it will never be realized.

- **Comprehensible:** To drive engagement, the strategy should present the challenges and the future in a way that makes it accessible to as many as possible, showing tangible improvements in everyday situations.

- **Actionable:** A strategy without a roadmap, or at least a list of actions, will have no effect. Value cannot be added until the actions identified are carried out in line with the strategy.

- **Consensus:** A strategy must gather and channel the energy of many people to create the desired impact. If the employees or various initiatives within an organization pull in different directions, this will lead to a tug-of-war that either slows progress to a crawl or prevents it completely.

4.1.3   AN AGILE AND INCLUSIVE STRATEGY PROCESS

The complex, rapidly changing world around us is unlikely to become simpler or slow down anytime soon. Therefore, a strategy cannot account for everything. Instead, it needs to focus on what is most important and be updated regularly. Extensive strategy efforts with long time horizons end up becoming irrelevant before they are even finished. Therefore, it is essential to identify the most important areas and strive to take actions that quickly create value and unlock new insights.

Here, we present a methodical albeit pragmatic approach to creating a digital workplace strategy based on these guiding principles:

- A cross-functional working group that co-creates the strategy from a holistic view of the digital workplace.
- The users are put front and center, with a clear focus on adding value by directly or indirectly involving users in strategy development.
- The strategy is iterated in a clear and simple manner with the help of tangible visual models.

Strategy development should be seen as an ongoing process, as illustrated in Figure 37. After the first version of the strategy is created (version 1.0), regular updates (version 1.1, 1.2, and so on) are made to implement corrections or incorporate new experiences in relevant areas. When the strategy is eventually reviewed as a whole, this leads to a new major version of the strategy (version 2.0).

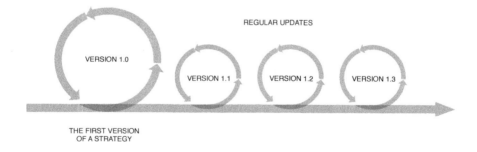

Figure 37. An iterative strategy development process.

Working on a strategy in a number of short and fast iterations reduces the time it takes to get started on projects and activities that add value while also necessitating a focus on what is most important for putting forward a viable strategy. The capability to test and draw conclusions on whether assumptions, priorities, and decisions are right or wrong at an early stage is important.

Strategy development usually has many starting points depending on factors such as the size and maturity of the organization. In a small organization, it's natural for the entire business to be considered in strategy development. In large organizations, we have positive experiences starting with an overall strategy driven from the top. This can then be applied and specified for various business domains and functions, or vice versa, when a business domain is more of a driving force and can see great value in creating a digital workplace strategy.

In this case, the first version of the strategy is created and used as a basis for strategy development to be continued and supplemented at the top. The most important thing is to move forward and produce results, even if the conditions are not perfect.

We develop the strategy step by step, defining, organizing, and analyzing key issues for the digital workplace. Five main steps are repeated during each iteration of the strategy (Figure 38).

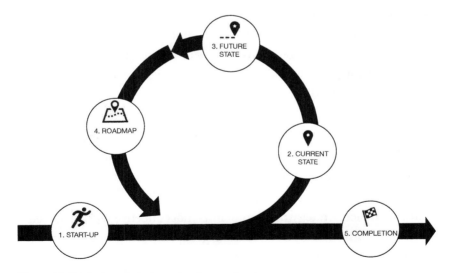

Figure 38. Each step of strategy development.

The main activities in each step are described briefly below:

1. **Start-up:** The first step is to determine the scope and direction for strategy development. The necessary documentation is also prepared during this step in close collaboration with the key stakeholders.

2. **Current state:** In the current state step, we gain an understanding of the conditions for the digital workplace by mapping the current state of the business, existing challenges, and capabilities in a clear and easily accessible manner.

3. **Future state:** The future state is then specified using supporting goals and priorities. Here, it is important to sketch the future state and make new opportunities tangible, which are manifested in ways of working and solutions within the digital workplace.

4. **Roadmap:** The next step is to identify the gap between the current and future state (gap analysis). The point here is to find various ways of closing the gap. This will result in a number of activities that we enter into a roadmap. Then, we assign ownership for each activity and for the roadmap as a whole.

5. **Completion:** Finally, the results are presented and discussed with relevant stakeholders. This is also when we decide on how we will work going forward and if any additions need to be made.

In our experience, strategy development is most effective when pursued in workshop form with a select working group. Utilizing time-boxed workshops creates continuous forward motion. The participants can then focus on the most important issues while the workshops help build consensus and garner support.

If needed, stakeholders with supplementary skills or perspectives can be invited to create synergies and add value. This can also be done on a large scale with the help of digital collaboration platforms. Nevertheless, strategy development will still largely have to be driven forward by a dedicated working group actively participating in and contributing to the workshops.

4.2 THE DIGITAL WORKPLACE CANVAS

To get started and avoid the risk of the organization acting like the six blind men and the elephant, it first needs to obtain a common holistic view of the digital workplace, both in terms of what it looks like now and how it should look in the future.

> *Understanding a business model requires not only knowing the compositional elements, but also grasping the interdependencies between elements. This is easier to express visually than through words. This is even more true when several elements and relationships are involved.*[39]

– Alexander Osterwalder, author and consultant

The lack of a holistic view is in fact the cause of many of the problems that characterize today's digital work environments. To solve these problems, we must gain an overview of the entire digital workplace and use this to build consensus and enable coordination. The overview needs to show the most important aspects – what we call "building blocks" – and how they relate to each other. This involves what the organization needs to know and have in place to develop the digital workplace in the right direction.

We took inspiration from Alexander Osterwalder's Business Model Canvas to create a canvas that helps give us a clear way of describing the most important building blocks in a digital workplace.

---

39 Alexander Osterwalder and Yves Pigneur, *Business Model Generation: A Handbook for Visionaries, Game Changers, and Challengers* (John Wiley & Sons, 2010).

Figure 39 presents a simplified image of the canvas and how all the components relate to one another.

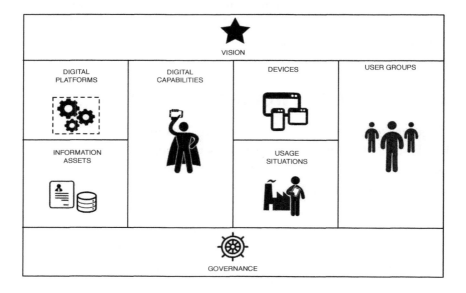

Figure 39. A canvas for the digital workplace.

The canvas becomes a gathering point around which others can get a sense of the bigger picture, discuss issues, and make decisions. Having one canvas for the current state and another for the future state makes it easy to shed light on the gap between them. The canvas describes a digital workplace from three main perspectives:

- **Management:** Vision and goals, governing principles, and responsibility.
- **Demand:** The users, their needs, and their touchpoints with the digital workplace via various devices in a variety of usage situations.
- **Delivery:** Digital capabilities, supporting digital platforms, and important information assets needed to meet demand.

The canvas is meant to be applied to an entire organization. However, it can naturally also be used for more narrowly defined areas such as a business unit, a process, or even a project. This could be a way to get the ball rolling by testing the canvas and this way of working while also generating broader interest in and a greater understanding of each part of the canvas.

When creating the strategy, the canvas is used to compile and communicate the answers to several key questions listed here under each component.

Vision
- How can the overall mission and vision be formulated in a way that sets the boundaries and direction for developing the digital workplace?
- What are the goals for the digital workplace?

User groups
- What are the most important user groups, and what are their distinguishing characteristics?
- What does each user group want and need to be able to perform and experience?

Devices
- What types of devices do the users need in various usage situations?
- What devices best meet the needs and match the working styles of the users?

Usage situations
- What usage situations are the users in when they need access to digital services?
- How do the users normally need to be able to move from one usage situation to another?

Digital capabilities

- What possibilities should the digital workplace offer users?
- What digital capabilities (digital services and ways of working) will meet the needs of the user groups?

Digital platforms

- What digital platforms are needed to provide the digital capabilities and services required?
- What is required for the digital platforms and services, both internal and external, to interoperate well?

Information assets

- What information assets do the users need?
- How can content with high findability and quality be provided?

Governance

- Who owns the digital workplace, and who is responsible for each of its parts?
- What principles guide decisions on the development of the digital workplace?

The most important answers to these questions are entered on the canvas. How much and in what form depend in part on the size of the organization. Small organizations naturally have space for more details while large organizations must present summarized information. Some choose to fill the canvas with post-its or simple lists. Others put more energy into images and visualizations. It's up to each organization to determine what adds the most value based on the circumstances. However, it's important to use a format that makes it easy to both read and update the content.

4.3   STEP 1 – START-UP

This step is about kicking off strategy development and building momentum through the early identification of the stakeholders within the organization who see a value in the strategy and are interested in its realization.

4.3.1   FORMING THE WORKING GROUP

The first item on the agenda is to bring in several people who can devise the strategy. In our experience, an effective way of getting results quickly is to appoint a working group of enthusiastic and driven employees that is relatively small in number yet broad in terms of skills and experience. Although we will need to involve many more people to ensure the strategy is effective, supported, and realizable, this working group will do the heavy lifting.

What determines the actual number of people that should compose the working group? This may vary depending on the organization's digital maturity and size, and what parts require extra engagement and support. A working group of 7 to 12 people usually works best for effective workshops and balanced results.

Even if a working group does most of the work, strategy development must be transparent to the extent that other stakeholders can see what is being done and why. This is done by openly sharing what activities are in the works and their aim followed by regular briefings on their progress. This enables the understanding of and support for the strategy to be secured among a large number of employees. Then those who are not members of the working group can be involved, for example, by enabling them to ask questions, contribute ideas and stories, and confirm or challenge various assumptions and conclusions. This also enables the identification of potential ambassadors within the organization who will play a key role in implementing the strategy.

The working group must incorporate a number of skills. In addition to a fundamental understanding of the digital workplace and service-dominant logic, which we review earlier in this book, the group must possess knowledge and experience from a wide variety of domains.

Business development
The group needs to have the ability to create a link to other business strategies, formulate a robust vision, set important goals for the digital workplace, and identify potential improvements to ways of working.

Experience design
In addition to experience with user research and needs analysis, the group should know how to identify important digital workplace characteristics, user touchpoints with multiple digital devices, and usage situations relevant to the employees.

Information management
This includes proficiency in taking inventory of information assets and understanding content processes in order to find, create, manage, and share information. Insights into information structures, formats, categorization, and quality are other key knowledge domains.

Platforms and architecture
Familiarity with various digital platforms, business-wide architecture issues, and service orientation is a key requirement. Experience in modern IT development and delivery processes is also a plus.

Management and governance
It is crucial that the working group know how to accommodate various stakeholders, lead workshops, ensure continuous progress, and sketch plans. The realization of strategies and proposals requires the capability to prepare for changes in governance models and support the implementation of new digital ways of working.

Therefore, the working group must be composed of individuals with cross-functional skills who are capable of viewing problems and solutions holistically. Unfortunately, we see that strategy development is far too often managed by a group with skills from only one or a couple of domains. Very rarely does the group include participants who are representative of "typical" users or from user-supporting roles. If the skills cannot be found within the organization, this alone poses a challenge. The organization may then need further training, support from external experts, or closer collaboration with network forums that share experiences with organizations tackling similar challenges.

4.3.2   MAPPING THE STAKEHOLDERS

To make its implementation possible, support for the strategy must be secured from relevant stakeholders within the organization. To be able to do this, these stakeholders must first be identified, and their impact on the digital workplace and strategy development must be assessed.

Users and support functions
The users and the organization around the users are naturally key stakeholders for the digital workplace. User representatives must therefore be involved in strategy development at an early stage. These should be individuals who have a keen interest in and are early adopters of new technology and ways of working. One advantage of involving user representatives in strategy development is that they can help drive innovation and serve as role models. They also play a key role in answering questions and providing practical support to their colleagues.

On the basis of the users and their representatives, we can see three distinct categories of stakeholders that should be involved in strategy development.

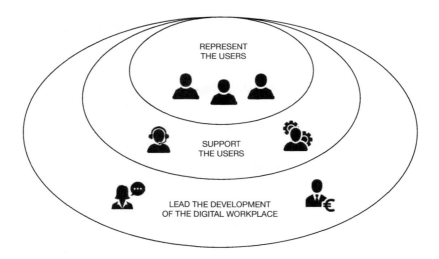

Figure 40. Stakeholder categorization model

Represent the users
The roles that represent users in the capacity of ambassadors or other representatives are included here. These roles are familiar with the day-to-day conditions of the digital work environment.

Support the users
This category is home to the roles that support the users, such as support staff, trainers, or those responsible for user forums, websites, and so on. They have valuable insight into how well digital services are used and function in practice because they regularly meet the users and address their questions and needs. They are usually further down in the organization's hierarchy, which may explain why they are rarely involved in strategy development to the extent they should be.

Lead the development of the digital workplace
Roles in this category lead or enable the digital workplace in the capacity of executives, department heads, and the like. These roles are needed to secure the time and resources for developing the strategy. They also serve as guarantors that the results will be put into practice.

Other common stakeholders

Executive roles and staff functions that usually see the value of or need to be actively involved in the development of the digital workplace are presented below.

Communications department

Communications department employees usually push for issues involving news, management information, and employee communications. They often take responsibility for the brand, user experience, and the availability and findability of business-critical information. Some communicators have also begun to see themselves as facilitators in terms of enabling and encouraging dialogue between individual employees and various cross-functional organizational groups.

Human Resources department

Those engaged in human resources issues often see a clear value in the digital workplace – it is a core part of the employees' work environment and a platform for building relationships, sharing knowledge, and serving as a culture bearer. The Human Resources department often comes up with initiatives that involve supporting increased learning, leadership development, and change management in the business..

Line managers and process owners

For line managers and process owners, the digital workplace is a platform for driving productivity increases in organizational units, processes, and at the individual level. This may involve automating tasks, decreasing administration, and reducing waste (non-value added activities), in part, by enabling self-service and providing a better basis for decision-making.

Business development

Those responsible for business development see the digital workplace as an arena for increased collaboration, both within the organization and with external parties. They also see it as infrastructure for innovation that brings people and ideas together across organizational boundaries and as a way of generating and driving engagement for new initiatives that strategically develop the business.

IT department

The IT department, a key stakeholder of the digital workplace, has a strong incentive to move toward a more cohesive and integrated digital workplace. Initiatives such as consolidating IT systems and creating service-centric, flexible digital platforms are often high on the agenda.

4.3.3   ENGAGING THE STAKEHOLDERS

To figure out which stakeholders are important to consider and engage with in the strategy process, it's a good idea to start with each of the categories described just before this section and brainstorm potential stakeholders. Then specify the roles of each stakeholder, their primary work, and the main challenges of their current positions.

Once the stakeholders have been identified, the next step is to determine how they should be considered in strategy development. This is done by asking the following questions:

- What significance does the strategy have to them, or what interest do they have in seeing the strategy realized?
- What influence do they have on the realization of the strategy, that is to say, making the necessary changes happen?

Figure 41 shows a matrix that can be used to answer these questions, with one axis for interest and another for influence.[40]

---

40 Based on a power/stakeholder matrix from James R. Gardner, Robert Rachlin, and Allen Sweeny, *Handbook of strategic planning* (John Wiley & Sons, 1986).

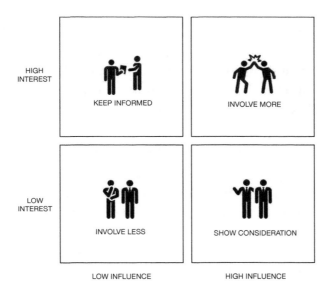

Figure 41. Interest-influence stakeholder matrix.

The matrix makes it easy to sort which stakeholders should be shown more or less consideration and who should be directly represented in strategy development:

- The stakeholders with high interest and high influence require maximum consideration and should be given the ability to participate. They are key players when it comes to getting things done.
- However, there's little point in spending time on and involving those with low interest and low influence.
- Those with high interest but low influence may be good to keep informed.
- It may be advisable to keep stakeholders with high influence but low interest satisfied so they do not get in the way of progress. However, there is no great reason to get them to actively contribute to the strategy process.

Stakeholder mapping helps the working group gain an understanding of who the strategy is created for and how it will be composed. Adding value for users is naturally at the heart of a digital workplace strategy, but achieving this requires that the most important stakeholders understand the strategy and actively support it. This is why it must be presented in a way that is tailored to them in order to stimulate decisions and actions.

4.3.4   COLLECTING RELEVANT DOCUMENTATION

During the start-up phase, the working group goes through the strategy process and plans the activities, working meetings, and deliveries of strategy development. Also, some of the key stakeholders are interviewed to give the working group a better idea of the various problems and challenges, and to obtain tips on relevant goals and solutions. During these interviews, it is advisable to ask:

- What role and place does the stakeholder have in the organization?
- What experience does the stakeholder have of similar strategy development?
- What primary direction should strategy development take?
- What trends and driving forces impact the digital workplace?
- How mature is the organization in terms of digitizing ways of working?
- What strategies, initiatives, and major projects in the organization does the strategy need to consider?

The stakeholders should also be asked to share relevant documentation, such as business strategies, organizational charts, process specifications, and specifications of services.

4.3.5   DEFINING TERMS AND BUILDING CONSENSUS

It is very important that as many stakeholders as possible, especially the working group participants and the key stakeholders, share a common view of what the digital workplace is and how the digital workplace relates to business strategies and other ongoing and planned initiatives.

Each of the participants in the working group likely has different views on and approaches to what a digital workplace is, why it must be developed, and what is important about it. This is why it's a good idea to prepare introductory documentation that defines key terms such as the digital workplace while also agreeing on why the digital workplace is important, who is impacted, and what primary capabilities it should provide.

Terms in relation to approaches and methodology, as described in this book, and business-specific terms should also be defined. It's enough to create a simple glossary and agree on the words and definitions in it. Knowing you are talking about the same thing when using a specific word is crucial to building consensus and avoiding unnecessary misunderstandings, both within the working group and in contact with the rest of the organization.

Everything is then summarized in a presentation the working group goes through and discusses based on the range of experiences and perspectives of the participants, and then it is made available to relevant stakeholders, preferably the entire organization. The importance of sharing a common view of what the digital workplace is and why it's needed to succeed in the work to come is something we cannot emphasize enough.

4.3.6   ALIGNING WITH BUSINESS STRATEGIES

The digital workplace strategy cannot be left hanging – it needs to be linked to other strategies or major ongoing and planned initiatives and programs within the business.

In the stakeholder section, we gave a few examples of functional domains with a direct bearing on the digital workplace, including communications, human resources, IT, and business development.

The working group now reviews the documentation collected and the interviews conducted during the start-up phase and extracts key terms and goals from them. The group describes them in brief and, if possible, specifies how they should be prioritized in relation to one another.

Real-world example

A government agency whose operations include innovation issues identified several parts of strategies for communications, human resources, business development, and IT that are directly related to the digital workplace. This was summarized into the following headings:

- Learning organization
- Findability and relevance
- Common ways of working
- Harmonized user experience
- Flexibility in change
- Consolidated platforms

They then prioritized these from one to three, with one being the most important.

4.3.7   FORMULATING THE MISSION AND VISION

The mission and vision of the digital workplace set the playing field
for how it needs to be developed going forward. Both the mission
and vision should be created jointly by the working group and key
stakeholders to secure support for them as early as possible.

The key stakeholders are rarely interested in practical details in strategy
development, but the mission and vision are of interest, as they are
directly linked to the value of the digital workplace. If they are left out
and support is not secured until later, there will be a risk that, at various
occasions, proposals will be scrapped, drawn out, or lead to a political
discussion, which eventually causes everything to fizzle out.

Formulating the mission
The purpose of the mission is to address what role the digital workplace
should play for the business without reference to contemporary trends
and technical concepts. It should be related to the organization's overall
mission and address three main questions:

- **Purpose:** What will be offered?
- **Target group:** Who does the offering target?
- **Medium:** How is the offering provided?

When formulating the mission of the digital workplace, it is
recommended that the working group take a closer look at the
organization's overall mission to see if and how it can be referred to. The
group should then brainstorm terms that address the main issues of the
mission. Subsequently organizing and prioritizing these terms will build
a foundation for summarizing and formulating the mission in a single
sentence.

The working group uses the template in Figure 42 to help formulate the mission.

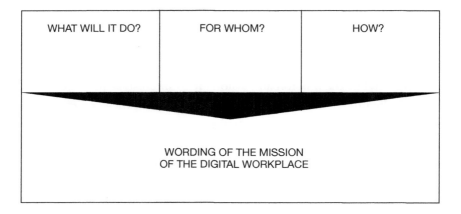

| WHAT WILL IT DO? | FOR WHOM? | HOW? |

WORDING OF THE MISSION
OF THE DIGITAL WORKPLACE

Figure 42. Template for formulating the mission of the digital workplace.

Real-world example

A multinational telecommunications company chose to formulate its mission for its digital workplace as follows:

"Enable communication and collaboration for employees and other contributors, through digital services."

Formulating the vision

The vision is a view of the future of the digital workplace, preferably more than five years away. In other words, the vision is something we strive to achieve with the digital workplace.

A good vision is distinguished by the following characteristics:

- It describes the desired future state of the digital workplace.
- It triggers a strong mental image in everyone who hears it.
- It motivates and interests people.
- It describes what they will be able to do, but not how.

A written description of the vision is not enough to fulfill these characteristics, so it should also be visualized appropriately. For example, we can visualize several scenarios that depict the employees and their working day when the future digital workplace is in place. However, a text-based version is sufficient at this stage. The vision is then made clearer and refined in the future state step.

Real-world example

The multinational telecommunications company formulated its vision as follows:

"An inspiring and collaborative digital workplace enabling innovation and engagement, everywhere."

The vision is put into words using an approach similar to that used to formulate the mission. The short text-based mission and vision statements are entered in the vision section of the canvas. Both should be seen as hypotheses that will be tested and will likely be revised slightly as well as made tangible during ongoing strategy development. Now that the mission and vision have been formulated, we have a direction in which to develop the strategy going forward, which begins with mapping the current state.

4.4   STEP 2 – CURRENT STATE

To gain an understanding of the current situation of the digital workplace within the organization, it's important that the working group assess the maturity of the organization and its levels of ambition. Where does it stand today in terms of the digital work environment? What levels of ambition should it have? What parts are important to build on?

4.4.1   ASSESSING THE ORGANIZATION'S MATURITY

A *maturity model* enables us to quickly obtain an understanding of where the organization's digital workplace currently stands, what direction it should develop in, and what is required to get there step by step. In Figure 43, we show a simple *maturity matrix* that has proven effective for starting discussions on an organization's maturity.[41]

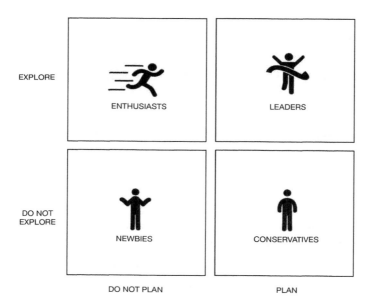

Figure 43. Maturity matrix for assessing an organization's maturity.

---

41   Inspired by the maturity model in Andrew McAfee, Didier Bonnet, and George Westerman, *Leading Digital: Turning Technology Into Business Transformation* (Harvard Business Review Press, 2014).

The main purpose of the maturity matrix is to see where the organization stands as a whole. However, it can also be applied on a smaller scale to departments, groups, and even individuals.

The vertical axis of the maturity matrix shows the degree to which people within the organization explore new digital services and technology. The horizontal axis shows the degree to which people within the organization plan digital management and organization. We often find that the exploratory axis represents a more competitive and results-focused culture, which is common in entrepreneurial organizations. Correspondingly, the planning axis represents a more structured and efficiency-focused culture, which is common in more administrative types of organizations such as government agencies and municipalities.

The four fields of the maturity matrix describe four *maturity profiles*. The profiles in turn are divided into five subareas: vision, ways of working, experience, technology, and governance. The maturity profile in each of these subareas is in one of the following steps:

- Reactive and "crawling" forward with various initiatives in the area because it must.
- Off to a start and actively "walking" forward with various coordinated initiatives in the area.
- Faster pace and "running" forward with proactive efforts to realize new digital opportunities.

Let's take a closer look at the four maturity profiles and what the maturity model looks like for each of them.

Newbies

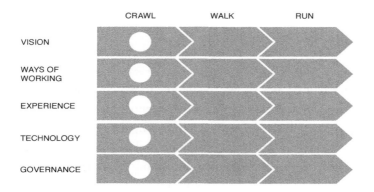

Figure 44. Maturity profile for newbies.

Newbies often have little understanding of the value of the digital workplace and may be skeptical of new digital opportunities and ways of working. The user experience is complex and fragmented for the most part. Some experimentation with new digital technology may occur, but it is more the exception than the rule. Governance is nonexistent because there is no common vision or idea to work toward.

Enthusiasts

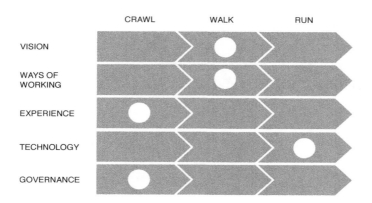

Figure 45. Maturity profile for enthusiasts.

Enthusiasts are characterized by advanced digital technology scattered out in different places throughout the organization but with little cumulative value due to a lack of coordination. Among them are individuals and groups with digital skills and understanding for new ways of working, but they have no common overall vision to work toward. The user experience is usually technology-focused and fragmented. Instead of being coordinated, governance takes different forms in different groups.

Conservatives

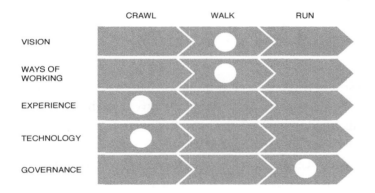

Figure 46. Maturity profile for conservatives.

Conservatives often have a vision, but it is underdeveloped. Some activities are pursued to increase digital skills and establish common ways of working, but the user experience is not put front and center and is complex and ineffective. They do have digital platforms, but new digital services and devices are not used. Governance is often elaborate and is exercised across organizational groups. Once the organization has decided on a digital initiative, it is usually coordinated with a focus on implementation issues.

Leaders

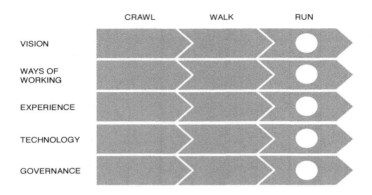

Figure 47. Maturity profile for leaders.

Leaders have a strong vision with clear business goals that is followed up and developed continuously. The user groups have the skills and understanding required for new efficient and flexible ways of working, and the user experience is steered toward simplicity and uniformity. Innovative digital services are found here, and their usage rate is high. The digital platforms are integrated, and governance provides clarity and results across the business.

The working group begins the maturity analysis of its own organization by attempting to position it in the maturity matrix, in other words, find what profile it fits best. Thereafter, the group assesses maturity in each subarea: vision, ways of working, experience, technology, and governance. Finally, the conclusions of the working group are substantiated with specific examples, preferably with quotations from the interviews with key stakeholders.

Also, it is often valuable to assess where key competitors or other comparable organizations stand in the maturity model. How is our own ambition level influenced by what others do? What is the time frame for our aims to be realized?

Following the maturity analysis, the working group should have already formed an opinion of what direction the organization needs to move in and what critical areas need to change for it to get there.

It is now time to begin working on the current state canvas. The first step is to obtain an understanding of demand, in other words, what support employees need from their digital workplace.

A continuous push forward is needed for strategy development to succeed, and that's why it is important not to get hung up on details while mapping the current state. Given that strategy development is iterative in nature, additional or more in-depth information can be added later. A more detailed inquiry is only required at this stage in the event of substantial knowledge gaps or uncertainty in some areas.

4.4.2   MAPPING THE DEMAND

The demand is mapped by identifying and describing groups of users (user groups) and their needs. We define *user groups* here as employees with similar needs and expectations of the digital workplace and its services. A starting point for finding user groups is user segments (broadly defined user groups) such as leaders, specialists, administrators, and field workers (Figure 48).[42]

SPECIALISTS   LEADERS   FIELD WORKERS   ADMINISTRATORS

Figure 48. Common user segments.

Each user segment typically has different tasks and working styles, which we will briefly summarize.

---

42   Based on Le Clair, C. (2011). *Best Practices: Developing an ECM/BPM strategy.* Forrester.

Leaders

Leaders can be managers, salespeople, or similar leading figures within the organization who are often on the move, both internally and externally, visiting customers or partners, and attending conferences or similar events. Additionally, they are activity-driven, with a strong focus on communication and relationship building.

Specialists

Some examples of specialists are advisors, designers, and engineers. They spend a great deal of time working in a stationary position producing information and solving complex tasks, but they are also on the move participating in meetings and meeting colleagues. They usually work in projects and collaborate with each other regularly.

Administrators

Common examples of administrators are accounting coordinators and assistants of various types. They also mostly work in a stationary position and mainly in structured processes where they follow various routines.

Field Workers

Field workers are people who work "out on the floor" (not behind a desk) or need to move to different locations to perform their work. Some examples include store staff, service technicians, and nurses. Their working days are often dominated by interaction with other people, problem-solving, and other routine tasks.

A starting point for identifying user groups is to list various *business roles* within the organization. Then, a *segmentation model* can be used to roughly sort the roles with similar tasks and behaviors into user groups. It's not uncommon to end up with approximately 6 to 12 main user groups. Identifying and sorting a manageable number of user groups makes it easier to think strategically about their needs and priorities.

The next step is to create *user group profiles* for each user group (Figure 49).

DESCRIPTION:		
ROLE:		
TASKS	DEVICES	SUCCESS FACTORS
WORKING STYLES	USAGE SITUATIONS	

Figure 49. User group profile template.

If you're familiar with personas, which we touch upon in chapter 4, you may be wondering why we use user group profiles instead of personas in the strategy development process. The reason is simple – a user group profile is not only a good starting point for user analysis but also a valuable tool for setting user-centered strategic priorities.

User group profiles and personas are both grounded in research. For identifying what personas to develop, user group profiles are particularly useful. While a user group profile provides a quantitative understanding of a group of users and describes ranges of characteristics for the entire group, a *persona* specifies a fictional individual with specific characteristics (for example, "Lisa Smith, a 31-year-old woman working as a sales manager in London"). The persona represents a group of users and highlights important characteristics of that group. As realistic representations of intended users, personas help build understanding and empathy for the intended users in the service development process.

Typical tasks are listed in the user group profiles, for example, whether the focus is on various types of process or knowledge work, and other parameters typical of the user group in question. For instance, it could be that they often have interactions with customers on sensitive subjects in public spaces, which requires special consideration for personal privacy and confidentiality.

What usage situation the user group is usually in and what digital devices the user group normally has access to are also specified in the user group profile. The same applies to success factors for the user group to succeed in their work, such as always having a stable internet connection.

Finally, the working group adds what have been identified as the most important user groups and most common usage situations and devices to the current state canvas.

Even if there are participants in the working group with profound knowledge of the business, the user groups identified and described should be considered hypotheses until they have been verified with representatives from each user group. This can be done by interviewing some people who represent each user group. The interviews also provide the opportunity to gain a more in-depth understanding of the user groups and their needs and conditions.

4.4.3   MAPPING THE DELIVERY

Once an initial understanding of demand has been obtained, it's time to map how the organization currently meets this, in other words, its delivery capability. The main point is to map digital capabilities and how well existing digital platforms and information assets meet the needs of the user groups.

Briefly and simply put, a *capability* means "being able to do something". We see a digital capacity as a collection of digital services with associated ways of working that make it possible for employees to perform a certain type of activity, such as finding expertise or co-creating documents with other employees.

It's important to realize that both the services and the ways of working must function in just the right way for the capability to be as strong as possible. An organization can provide many good digital services, which, for example, make it easier for employees to quickly find the expertise they're looking for, but if used incorrectly, the capability will not be as strong as it could be. We have identified a number of common basic capabilities and organized them into five categories (Figure 50) to make it easier to identify digital capabilities.

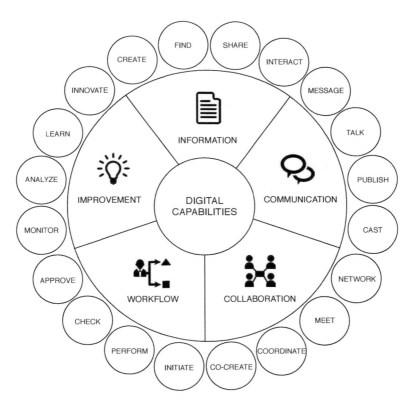

Figure 50. Key digital capabilities for the digital workplace.

Information

Information capabilities involve the support that is available for personal and collective information production, management, and consumption.

- **Create:** Produce or capture content by writing, scanning, recording, or the like.
- **Find:** Actively search, navigate, or discover relevant content, expertise, and resources.
- **Share:** Make a file or content available through a shared storage space.
- **Interact:** Consume content or add to its value by describing, organizing, or commenting on it.

Communication

Communication capabilities enable conversing and information sharing.

- **Message:** Send content, once or as part of a thread, to one or more people.
- **Talk:** Talk to one or more people at a certain point in time.
- **Publish:** Make an edited page or a quality-assured document available to one or more people.
- **Cast:** Stream audio or video to one or more people.

Collaboration

Collaboration capabilities involve support for developing relationships, sharing knowledge, and coordinating work.

- **Network:** Establish and develop relationships with other people.
- **Meet:** Interact with multiple people at a specific time and place.
- **Coordinate:** Lead, coordinate, and follow up work.
- **Co-create:** Produce content jointly with others.

Workflow

Workflow capabilities involve how well workflows are supported and how administration can be avoided through automation and self-service.

- **Initiate:** Start a sequence of fully or partially automated activities.
- **Perform:** Perform an activity by contributing information.
- **Check:** Review and monitor an activity in a workflow.
- **Approve:** Accept and set results of a workflow.

Improvement

Improvement capabilities involve creating the conditions to develop and improve ways of working, skills, information, ideas, and other assets.

- **Monitor:** Follow and be aware of events around you to act on.
- **Learn:** Access content for developing skills.
- **Analyze:** Compile content as a basis for insights and decisions.
- **Innovate:** Create, develop, and implement new ideas and concepts.

These are basic capabilities that can be used in various processes and business domains, such as marketing, sales, production, communications, HR, or finance. They also play a key role in the less structured yet increasingly important knowledge work performed in a business.

Thus, the same digital capability can be used for many different tasks and in many different usage situations, such as finding expertise or holding meetings. This also means that minor improvements to a digital capability can have a large overall impact on the organization's productivity, agility, and innovativeness.

Real-world example

The employees of an international construction company perceived their digital work environment as ineffective, fragmented, and to a certain degree, stressful. It was also designed more for document-based desk work than for flexible information sharing, collaboration, and innovation.

When we mapped and analyzed their existing digital capabilities, we found that they had been developed in different ways, for different purposes, in different time periods, and by different organizational groups.

For example, many processes and tasks were still largely dependent on hard copies in the form of documents such as drawings, contracts, and project plans. This created very real problems prior to moving to a new activity-based office with minimal options for storing physical binders, folders, and documents.

Their strongest digital capability relative to the others was communication, with a business-wide intranet that includes standardized publishing and personalization procedures. Employees also had the capability to blog, share videos, chat, and make conference calls. However, no one took overall responsibility for the user experience because these parts were all managed by different departments. In other words, they did not get the maximum value from the substantial investments they made in processes and digital platforms.

4.4.4   MAPPING DIGITAL CAPABILITIES

Now it is time to map the organization's digital capabilities. The template in Figure 51 is used to stimulate a discussion within the working group.

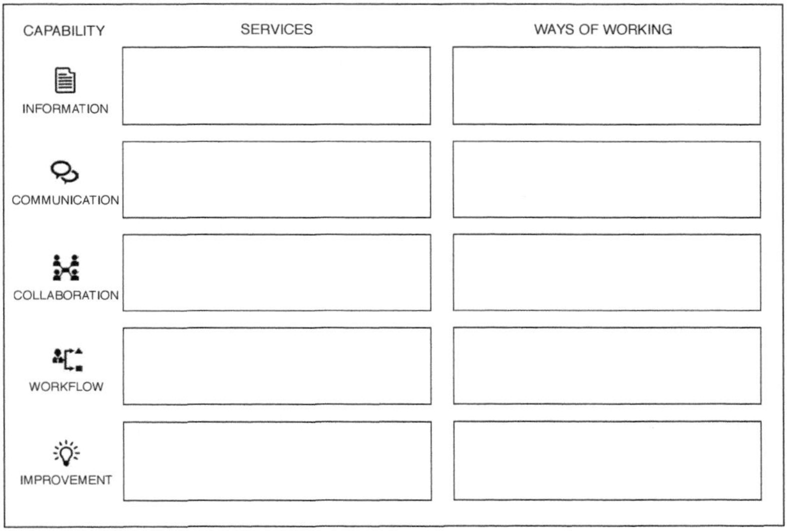

Figure 51. Template for documenting digital capabilities.

To fill in the template, the working group asks questions such as:

- What services are currently supported in each capability, and how well do they work?
- Are there common ways of working that are effective for communication, collaboration, and the other capabilities?
- Does the organization suffer from waste, ineffective behaviors, or obstructive attitudes?
- Do employees work as productively as possible with the right digital services and support?

The working group also takes the opportunity to write down the problems and challenges it sees in the current state.

What ideas and proposals are there for developing the capabilities? What can be done better, and what potential is there for adding business value?

The group writes the answers in the template. Then it assesses how well each capability currently works by rating them using numbers (1–5), colors (red–yellow–green), or a similar system.

Finally, the working group enters the digital capabilities along with their rating on the current state canvas.

4.4.5   MAPPING DIGITAL PLATFORMS

A *digital platform* is a type of packaging or grouping of functionalities. The digital services used within a business can be realized on several different digital platforms.

Comparing digital platforms with each other can be difficult. For example, what one provider chooses to call a "portal" may differ in functionality compared with what another provider has packaged under the same name. If you choose to use a specific provider's definition, it may create problems when it's time to switch to another provider with another definition. In this case, the new puzzle piece, to put it simply, is shaped differently and does not fit into the digital workplace.

To do our best to avoid this puzzle piece issue, we use a model (Figure 52) for digital platforms that is independent of suppliers but can be linked to various supplier offerings.

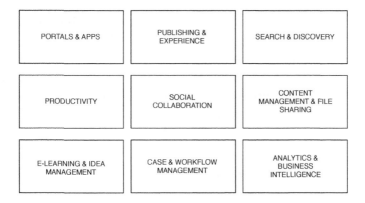

Figure 52. Model for mapping digital platforms.

Portals and apps

Portals give users access to a bundle of digital services all in one place. They manage logins and privileges and facilitate personalization and integration with underlying systems. The development of apps and self-service solutions is often supported. In some cases, the portal can also host marketplaces and e-commerce solutions.

Publishing and experience

Publishing and experience platforms help editors and writers create, manage, deliver, and customize content. These platforms make it possible to review and control the relevance and user experience of the content in various channels and devices. They also facilitate the process of creating and running campaigns for various user groups and connect them to external social media platforms.

Search and discovery

Search and discovery platforms help users find the information they need among various sources of content. These platforms include support for organizing content, providing navigation systems, and optimizing searches. Also, they usually include the functionality to give recommendations on relevant content.

Social collaboration
Traditional collaboration platforms usually provide functionality and services such as email, messaging, and calendaring along with support for online conferencing, meetings, and shared workspaces. Social collaboration platforms also provide functionality for social networking, blogs, and wikis. In addition, they usually provide functionality for allowing users to comment, follow, and share content with others.

Productivity
Productivity platforms provide functionality for creating and designing content in the form of documents, presentations, spreadsheets, mind maps, videos, and more. Recently, they have been designed with an increasingly strong link to social collaboration.

Content management and file sharing
Content management platforms support the process of capturing, creating, storing, delivering, and archiving content of various types. This may involve managing documents, images, videos, and other media. They also provide personal information management of documents and files with support for sharing them with others.

E-learning and idea management
Idea management platforms are used to generate, refine, vote on, and evaluate ideas. The ideas can be driven by contests and challenges, and sometimes support is included for the process of realizing the ideas. E-learning platforms include the capability to present, curate, and evaluate content and skills in various subject domains. This usually relies on a mix of IRL meetings, digital materials, and interactive tests.

Case and workflow management
Case management platforms mainly involve the capability to create workflows and automate processes in relation to various cases. Support is often included for monitoring events and managing outcomes based on set rules. Some platforms also provide support for modeling and simulating business processes.

Analytics and business intelligence

Analytics and business intelligence platforms enable the collection and compilation of transaction data and data on user interactions. This data is compiled and reported in well-organized instrument panels and reports, enabling the user to dig deep into various indicators and metrics in order to draw conclusions and make decisions. Sometimes these platforms include artificial intelligence functionality to process data, discover patterns, and make forecasts based on these patterns.

Choosing supplier offerings that complement one another can be challenging, and getting away from some overlap in functionality between digital platforms can be difficult. In such a case, it is extra important to be clear about and agree on ways of working – in other words, which functionality from what platform will be used for what tasks, and how?

Using the model in Figure 52 to map their systems is a way of positioning the digital platforms within the organization in relation to one another and a way of gaining a better understanding of how they complement and potentially overlap with one another. The model can also be used to make note of and identify the following:

- Various challenges and problem areas
- Ongoing projects and initiatives
- Separate areas of responsibility and ownership
- Strategic choices and technical alternatives

A common model for the digital platforms lays the foundation for the organization to set better requirements for and collaborate better with its providers. It also simplifies how architectonic challenges are managed, such as consolidation and integration needs. Finally, the model helps show what investments are suitable to make and what new initiatives may need to be started.

When mapping current digital platforms, the working group uses the model and lists the systems and tools the organization has in each category. If multiple versions of the same platform or tool are used in parallel, such as SharePoint 2013 and SharePoint 2016, these should be listed. The working group also takes the opportunity to pick up on any problems and make a note of any proposals and ideas on how digital platforms can be improved and interoperate better.

If an organization has a small number of digital platforms, the working group lists those that are most important on the current state canvas. Otherwise, it's enough to enter what types of digital platforms the organization has and how many competing platforms there are in each type. For example, one company we worked with had over 60 different CRM systems. Instead of listing each and every one of them, we entered the number of CRM type systems.

4.4.6 MAPPING INFORMATION ASSETS

Information can be seen as the fuel of a business. A fuel that powers communication, collaboration, knowledge sharing, and business processes of various types. But what information is so important that the engine of the business can gain or lose speed, or even come to a complete stop, if the fuel is not available or of poor quality? The identification of these information assets with significant business value plays a key role in strategy development.

Content is something that conveys information, for example, images, diagrams, videos, and text in various forms (documents, web pages, and data are most common). Today, many organizations experience uncontrolled growth of digitally created content. This in turn often results in employees struggling to find, share, and reuse content in order to make use of the information it conveys.

Identifying content by format

So, what can you do to see the forest for the trees? One approach
is to identify the main content formats of the business: web pages,
documents, and data. Traditionally, digital platforms have specialized in
one of these formats.

Web pages

A web page is a document that can be read and interpreted by a web
browser and has a unique address so it can be found, linked to, and
shared. Web pages may include text, images, and videos, and they are
organized into websites. Episerver and Sitecore are just two examples
of providers of digital platforms for creating, managing, and publishing
content to web pages and for managing websites.

Documents

A document is a collection of information or data stored under a file
name in a file system. It may contain a presentation, spreadsheet, book,
or notes. Content is created by domain experts or employees in various
positions. Microsoft and EMC are two examples of providers of digital
platforms for managing documents.

Data

Data is some kind of fact or value that can be processed by people or
machines but has not yet been interpreted and composed into something
meaningful and usable, that is to say, information. Data can be found in
various databases in the form of tables, forms, and spreadsheets. Data is
created by employees or generated by automated transactions, analyses,
and sensors. SAP and Oracle are examples of providers of digital
platforms that manage data.

Identifying content by usage context

A supplementary perspective to the content format is to look into what purpose the information conveyed by the content is intended to fulfill, which we call the usage context. Figure 53 shows some general usage contexts common to all industries and types of businesses.

Figure 53. General usage contexts for content.

Management
Management information is information intended to steer the business in a certain direction and is usually geared toward all employees or various groups within the organization. Examples of content containing management information include news, strategy documents, policy documents, and company reports.

Process
Process information is information intended to govern how a sequence of activities will be performed and what results they will generate. Examples of content that conveys process information include product models, drawings, process diagrams, and standard operating procedures.

Collaboration
Collaboration within organizational groups and projects can be seen as another usage context. Examples of content employees collaborate on include spreadsheets, presentations, meeting minutes, and various work

materials. In this context, the content can be seen as more informal, as it does not follow the same strict quality requirements as management and process information.

Personal
The individual employee both creates and uses content as part of their daily work in order to convey information to others. This type of content can be found in substantially larger volumes compared with more formal content because almost all employees continuously create new content on a daily basis.

Content that conveys management information and process information can be seen as more formal and usually must be quality assured through various review and approval procedures. This content is generally created by fewer employees than those who consume and use the content.

It is not unusual for management information in the form of news and business events to be considered the most important to publish to employees. This type of content is often featured prominently on the intranet. However, from the perspective of the typical employee, other information is more relevant and valuable in their daily work, such as information relating to the employee's role and tasks. A more user-oriented approach could thus dictate a change in priorities for what content is published and how.

Identifying collections of content
What then is a suitable level for inventorying the information assets in an organization without getting lost in the jungle of content? One challenge is gaining control over the large volume of content and its spread. Looking at collections of content rather than specific content enables you to create a clear map of the most important information assets. The content format is combined with the usage context in the template below, which shows some examples of various collections of web pages.

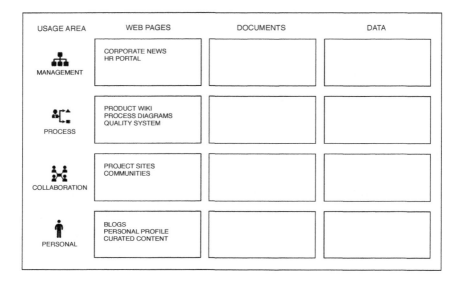

Figure 54. Content template with examples of collections of web content.

From the perspective of the user groups, it is important that the information they need can be found and used efficiently when and where it is needed. Most people don't care where the content that conveys this is stored or on what platform it is managed. Therefore, it is also relevant to measure and understand the findability and quality of the content conveying the information. If it is difficult to find the content, it will take longer for the employees to use the information in their work. If the quality of the content is poor, it will be difficult for employees to grasp and interpret the information correctly, which makes their work harder.

The working group now attempts to jointly identify what information assets are important in the business based on various content formats and usage contexts. To avoid being overwhelmed by the volume of the content, they should list the content collections instead of specific content.

The working group also considers whether there are known issues and challenges associated with the content and the information it conveys, for example, in terms of quality, security, access, and compliance. The content matrix enables the working group to identify whether ownership of the information assets is clear and whether the digital platforms used to manage the content are sufficient. As usual, the working group documents the proposed improvements and other ideas generated.

The most important content collections are then entered on the canvas marked by a number or color indicating what parts currently meet user needs best. When assigning these priorities, it is crucial to assess the content's findability and quality.

4.4.7 SPECIFYING ROLES AND RESPONSIBILITIES

The increasing complexity and fragmentation that characterizes the digital work environments of many organizations are among the consequences of when an organization lacks coordination. Those responsible for various IT systems have worked in silos and become blind to the whole. Therefore, we consider common holistic governance of the digital workplace to be necessary for coordinating and balancing various interests and change initiatives.

The organizations that lack coordinated governance often have strong business units and departments that more or less manage themselves in terms of IT investments. This leads to suboptimization and makes it impossible to create synergies. The IT-related initiatives implemented add relatively little value from a holistic view of the business. The gains achieved in one part of the business could very well be negated by losses in other parts of the business.

When the IT department steps forward to take a more coordinating role, it is often with an aim of achieving a more coherent IT delivery. This usually means simplifying through consolidation, enhancing the security, or increasing the cost efficiency of the IT delivery.

The challenge for the IT department in this case is to manage the many and often contradictory needs and priorities it encounters in different parts of the business.

Despite its coordination aims, the IT department is perceived as difficult, reactive, and in general, a stumbling block to change and innovation. We believe that this is because the IT department is usually far too focused on its own delivery and concentrates on stability and cost control instead of creating value for users and the business. Therefore, the governance of the digital workplace should be above the IT department, although it must be represented in the governance forums.

We believe that if the IT department is to be empowered to take a more proactive role in the digitalization of the business, then it needs a much clearer and more business-focused mission from management. We also believe that the IT department's mission should primarily involve enabling value creation, while each part of the business begins coordinating their planning, prioritization, and requirement specifications for IT investments.

What people and what roles actually have a responsibility related to the digital workplace? Here, we list four types of responsibility for the digital workplace from a holistic view and for each of the building blocks of the canvas:

- **Lead:** The roles that drive or lead work on the digital workplace or parts of it.
- **Approve:** The roles that make decisions and bear the ultimate responsibility for the digital workplace or parts of it.
- **Participate:** The roles that work on and take responsibility for deliveries to the digital workplace or parts of it.
- **Informed:** The roles influenced by decisions and deliveries, which therefore need to be informed of what is happening to the digital workplace or parts of it.

This model of responsibility, based on the RACI model (also called *responsibility assignment matrix*), is particularly useful for thinking across the business and organizational silos and can be applied regardless of how the business is currently organized.

The working group now uses the template in Figure 55 to identify who is responsible for (or should be responsible for) the digital workplace. The group tries to name the roles with the help of documentation collected from the start-up phase and their own experience of how this works in practice. If it turns out that responsibility is deficient, overlapping, or unclear, these are important insights to act on.

BUILDING BLOCK	LEAD	APPROVE	PARTICIPATE	INFORMED
OVERALL				
VISION				
USER GROUPS				
DEVICES				
USAGE SITUATIONS				
DIGITAL CAPABILITIES				
DIGITAL PLATFORMS				
INFORMATION ASSETS				

Figure 55. Responsibility template for the digital workplace.

The roles that approve the changes in the end are those with ultimate responsibility for the digital workplace, although they lead neither the strategy efforts nor the change efforts. We now list the roles in the governance section of the current state canvas.

4.4.8   PRIORITIZING PROPOSED IMPROVEMENTS

During its efforts to describe the current state, the working group has probably identified many problems and proposed solutions related to them. Given that these have been continuously documented, they can now be used to formulate the future state and the upcoming roadmap.

The working group now sorts through the proposed improvements to see if any immediate action can be taken. For each proposed improvement, we estimate the value – what it potentially could add for the business – and the amount of effort required for its implementation. The working group does this with the help of the prioritization matrix in Figure 56.

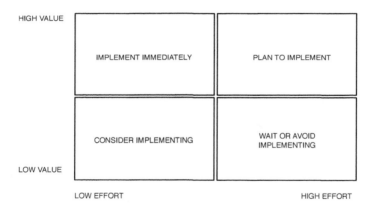

Figure 56. Prioritization matrix for actions.

This way, the working group can demonstrate that they do not always have their heads in the clouds when engaged in strategy development, but can in fact be down-to-earth and keen to generate fast business results. For each action of this type, it is important that the working group appoint someone who will be responsible for driving the improvement forward and specifying needs and solutions in detail. Once this is done, the participants can now turn their attention forward and start working on shaping the future state.

4.5   STEP 3 – FUTURE STATE

We're now ready to specify the future state of the digital workplace. The working group will use the canvas to review what trends and driving forces have influenced the digital workplace, make the vision tangible, and design a more attainable future state. Another key step is to gain more in-depth insights into the needs of the user groups because these are critical to how the digital workplace should function and be designed in the best way.

4.5.1   EXPLORING TRENDS AND DRIVING FORCES

The new digital opportunities that are continuously emerging merit closer observation and exploration. The working group therefore identifies and selects what driving forces and trends it considers the most important and influential in the digital workplace. At this point, it might be a good idea to ask questions such as these:

- What was revealed during the stakeholder interviews?
- What was mentioned in the documentation collected?
- Is there further information from external sources and reports that the working group is aware of?

Now it's time to harness the trends and driving forces identified by the working group to brainstorm ideas and to explore how to add business value. The ideas need not be realizable at this stage – it's more important that they stimulate free thinking. This in turn could lead to anything from simple improvements to more groundbreaking innovations.

One way of doing this is to brainstorm ideas around a prioritized trend or driving force such as artificial intelligence or smart agents. The ideas generated by the working group are then combined into a concept that is visualized and presented to the other participants of the group and other stakeholders. This process can then be repeated for other prioritized trends and driving forces.

Real-world example

An international construction company realized that digitalization would result in new ways of working not only for its employees but also in relation to its customers and partners. It knew that understanding and utilizing these new ways of working are prerequisites for remaining competitive in the future.

The construction company identified several driving forces and trends it determined were important in its aim to be more innovative. It also had the insight that increased innovativeness requires better support for knowledge work and collaboration among employees.

Therefore, the employees needed better possibilities to work more independently and flexibly with the help of a new digital workplace and a new physical office environment. These are the trends and driving forces that the construction company chose to focus on.

Activity-based offices
The construction company planned a new office that makes better use of office space and supports various ways of working productively, both individually and with others.

Knowledge work
Many of the core tasks of the business consisted of knowledge work. Systematic support for personal information management, collaboration, and innovation had previously not been given a great degree of attention.

Flexible work

Many employees work both inside and outside of the office, such as at construction sites and partner facilities, and needed access to services and information from these locations. It was also important to provide better support for various working styles and a better balance between work and leisure time.

ONE company

Much of the communication within the construction company was from management to the employees. The construction company determined that promoting a closer dialogue between employees and management was important, but even more important was ensuring stronger integration throughout the business by enabling new opportunities for employee communication and networking.

Reduced waste

The employees felt that the digital work environment increased their stress and cognitive load. Therefore, the company wanted to focus on reducing waste in digital processes and interactions with IT systems. Some examples of waste included storing the same information in multiple locations, managing information in hard copy, underusing available digital services, navigating complicated interfaces, and struggling to find and reuse existing information.

Digitalization

The construction company saw the potential to take advantage of new digital technology and new behavior patterns that emerged from digitalization and the use of social media, mobility, cloud services, web analytics, and the Internet of Things (IoT).

4.5.2   IDENTIFYING GUIDING PRINCIPLES

Well then, what digital capabilities should an organization invest in? Which ones add the most business value? And which ones could even send the business in the wrong direction?

Strategy is about making informed decisions that move something in the desired direction, in this case, the digital workplace. Therefore, choosing what not to do is just as important as choosing what to do. And with technical capabilities, conditions, behaviors, and expectations in a state of rapid and constant flux, we have to focus on finding a direction rather than knowing exactly what to do.

To make this type of decision, we need guiding principles to steer the development of the digital workplace in the right direction, regardless of what technology or other changes enable the move.

In addition to guiding principles, it is also advantageous to define what characteristics the digital workplace should have, such as being usable, secure, appealing, and seamless. Some of these were already identified when the text-based vision was created.

The guiding principles should relate to the values on which the organization wishes to build its business and how the business should change in the future. Examples of such guiding principles for the digital workplace are summarized below.

Openness
The value of information increases as more people use it for something useful to the organization. If it's locked away, it may be difficult to find. The digital workplace should take information that could be valuable to others within the organization and that is not subject to confidentiality requirements and allow it to be made available and easy to find for those who need it.

Transparency

Transparency means that, when finding information, employees can see where it came from, when it was created, by who, and find other related information. This also increases their trust in the information and will give them the confidence to act on it. A digital workplace that is transparent also makes the contributions of employees more visible and possible to acknowledge while also enabling the identification of valuable skills and information assets.

Participation

Participation involves enabling everyone with something to contribute to participate in communications. We often do not know in advance who has something valuable to contribute. Therefore, the digital workplace should be more inviting and encourage participation.

Dialogue

Dialogue allows us to quickly achieve a mutual understanding of something. The greater the possibilities for dialogue we have, the faster we can understand each other and put this understanding into practice. The digital workplace should make two-way communication easy in order to build mutual understanding, consensus, and engagement.

Acknowledgement

Acknowledgment is an important factor for fostering an open and communicative culture. Most of us are motivated by praise from others for what we do. If we receive praise for sharing information, ideas, and knowledge in an open and positive manner, we will be motivated to continue doing so. The digital workplace must encourage and make it easy for employees to acknowledge each other's contributions and to receive fast and clear feedback on their own contributions.

4.5.3   MAKING THE VISION TANGIBLE

Although we cannot say exactly what the digital workplace will look like in a future state and even less when the vision will be achieved, it's important to try to make the vision tangible. A tangible vision makes it easier to identify and specify a more achievable future state. It's also easier to see what's missing and what needs to be done to get there, in other words, a gap analysis between the current state and the future state. The actions contained in the gap analysis result in the roadmap we describe later in the chapter.

The text-based vision can be made tangible using various visualizations such as mockups and scenarios that illustrate how the digital work environment could look and how it will be used once the vision is achieved. These help to stimulate ideas about and explain the characteristics and guiding principles that will be added to the vision.

Another way of making the vision tangible is to imagine that the strategy has already been implemented and was successful, resulting in a cover story in a popular magazine.[43] A more vivid description of the vision can be made using illustrations and short texts (see Figure 60). We recommend brainstorming and sketching the following:

- **Cover:** Summarizes the success story.
- **Headings:** Puts words to key parts of the story.
- **Quotes:** Collects comments from the stakeholders, users, and other people of significance.
- **Facts:** Highlights interesting facts and goals achieved.
- **Models:** Can be used to explain important factors of the success.
- **Situations:** Provides examples of tangible improvements in day-to-day work.

---

43   James Macanufo and Sunni Brown, Gamestorming: *A Playbook for Innovators, Rulebreakers, and Changemakers* (O'Reilly, 2010).

As the basis for this task, the working group examines the trends and driving forces previously identified and the guiding principles and characteristics added to the vision.

Figure 57. Cover story exercise template.

4.5.4   DEFINING AND PRIORITIZING GOALS

With a more tangibly expressed vision, the working group now proceeds to set the goals for the future state.

We initially described the vision as something far into the future, at least five years away. In contrast, the future state should represent a more foreseeable future, say two or three years ahead. We use goals to make the future state more concrete. These goals help us zero in on and demonstrate the difference that will be made in the business once the future state is achieved – in other words, what has improved.

Real-world example

A government agency engaged in innovation issues conducted a goal exercise which led to the conclusion that the following goals were its highest priorities:

- The ability to find correct and relevant information faster.
- The ability to more easily work toward common goals and employ common ways of working.
- Increased participation and transparency in collaboration

The next highest priority was to increase knowledge sharing and skills transfer in internal and external networks and provide a more coherent portal to information and tools.

Having a starting point is naturally crucial to being able to see and measure success, in other words, how the digital work environment performed prior to the commencement of digital workplace development. Therefore, we should measure the goals that have been set before we begin to implement any improvements or actions.

A good starting point is to brainstorm goals based on what should "increase", "decrease", "be faster", "be simpler", "be better", and the like within the business. Once this is done, similar goals are grouped together so that their total number does not exceed ten. Keeping down the number of overall goal areas makes them easier to grasp as well as easier to communicate to others outside of the group.

After this, the working group formulates a sentence that describes each goal area. It also identifies specific metrics that clarify when the goal areas or goals have been achieved. This is followed by a joint assessment of the relevance of the goals.

The following questions can help when assessing the relevance of goals:

- Do the goals describe what we seek to achieve?
- Will we be satisfied if we achieve the goals?
- How will we know when we have achieved the goals? Give examples.
- Is it possible for the digital workplace to achieve this?
- Are these goals the most important goals for the digital workplace?
- Are the goals in line with the overall strategies, goals, and initiatives of the business?

Real-world example

The government agency defined the following metrics and ways of measuring to determine whether it actually succeeded in "being able to find and access correct and relevant information faster":

Metric	Measurement
The time it takes to find specific content by searching, navigating, or discovering.	Lab tests were selected as the main instrument of measurement.
The level of readability or relevance of specific content.	A combination of automatic readability indices and subjective reader ratings.

All goals cannot be equally important, and guidance on what goals take precedence over others is needed in the event of a conflict. Therefore, the goals are prioritized in relation to each other before they are entered in the vision section of the future state canvas.

4.5.5   PROFILING THE USER GROUPS

The digital workplace is essentially designed for the employees in order to meet their needs. The true value intended by the vision and goals is created when the digital workplace is used. The employees are represented by user groups in strategy development, which necessitates a strong understanding of who the user groups are, what needs they have, and what contexts and usage situations they are usually in when performing their work. It is not until this is clear that we can see what services they need and how they need to be designed.

The working group has already identified several user groups and specified them with user group profiles in the current state step. Now it's time to pose the question of whether they represent the user groups of the future as well. With the vision made clear and goals for the future state specified and prioritized, the user groups can be seen in a new light. It is a good idea to reflect over the following questions:

- What user groups are the most important to support based on the mission and vision of the digital workplace?
- How can the user groups, directly or indirectly, contribute to achieving the goals of the future state?
- What digital capabilities may be lacking to enable the attainment of these goals?

A new user group profile is created for new user groups. Once the most important user groups are identified, they are then prioritized based on their significance for achieving the goals. This prioritization has practical consequences.

Real-world example

For a government authority engaged in innovation, it was clear, based on the goals prioritized, that roles such as specialists with a high share of the knowledge work were a higher priority. They were thus given more attention in comparison to, for example, staff with more routine administrative tasks.

User groups that are added and their prioritization are listed on the future state canvas. The next question to ask is how the needs profile can be expanded and linked to delivery capability.

4.5.6   IDENTIFYING USER GROUP NEEDS

The digital workplace is designed to meet the needs of users, providing the best ways for them to perform their tasks and contribute to the business. But what will it provide to them, and how? Answering this question requires digging deeper into what the user groups need to be able to do and what they want to experience.

The working group should be composed in such a way that it has relatively strong insight into the needs of each user group. If this is the case, an initial estimate, or hypothesis, of the needs is made by the members of the working group. However, suitable representatives of the user groups must be interviewed to supplement and validate the needs profile.

More in-depth studies and specifications of user needs are undertaken during service development. The first priority during strategy development is to understand the overall needs profile.

To do this, we recommend asking two fundamental questions:

- What do the user groups want to do (or know)?
- What do the user groups want to experience (feel or avoid)?

Here, "doing something" refers to an activity that is related to the employee's work. This may involve an activity where the employee processes information, communicates or collaborates with others, does something as part of a workflow, or is involved in improvements.

As a user, the employee usually wants to have a positive experience, for instance, experiencing that it is easy to report time or feeling confident in the statistics presented in a report. Inconvenient logins or complex forms that the employee wants nothing to do with are examples of things that can cause a negative experience.

A *needs map* is useful to identify and nail down the needs of each user group (Figure 58).

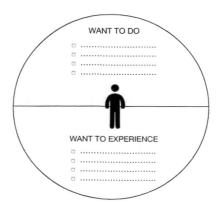

Figure 58. Needs map.[44]

The working group must use its experience of and insight into the needs of the user groups to attempt to answer what it thinks they want to be

---

44 Inspired by Osterwalder, A. Pigneur, Y. Bernarda, G. Smith A. Papadakos, T. (2014). *Value Proposition Design: How to Create Products and Services Customers Want.* Wiley.

able to do and experience in the future state. The following questions can be used to determine whether the most important needs of the user groups have been found:

- Will the user group be satisfied if these needs are met?
- If the needs are met, will this contribute to the attainment of the goals identified?

To obtain a solid basis for the work to come on the roadmap, the needs must also be prioritized in relation to the goals set. Instead of delving into what digital devices are best suited in different usage situations for a user group, it is more important at this stage to begin identifying what digital services and capabilities are required to meet the needs of the user groups.

4.5.7   IDENTIFYING DIGITAL SERVICES

A need can be met by employees gaining access to and using one or more digital services. The experience-based needs set the requirements for what characteristics the digital services should have. To do this in practice, we create an *offering map* for each user group (Figure 59).

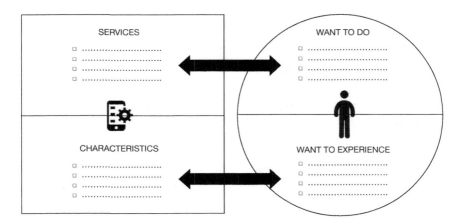

Figure 59. The connection between needs and offerings.

The offering map is inspired by the tool *Value Proposition Canvas*.[45]

Below are some examples from various needs and offering maps used in a client project.

Service	Want to do
News	See news from various parts of the business.
Business intelligence	Get help in gathering business intelligence.
Notes	Be able to make notes at meetings and share with colleagues.
File sharing	Be able to store and share content and files.
Time reporting	Be able to report time.

Characteristics	Want to experience
Mobile support	Be able to use services during inspections.
Easy access	Be able to access services without hassle.
Multi-device support	Be able to use their own computers and smartphones.
Easy to learn	Avoid time-consuming training.

By working through the needs maps for each user group, the working group can establish what services and characteristics they want and then list them in the offering maps. Given that the working group has prioritized the needs maps, it can now also make assumptions about how various services and characteristics should be presented. The working group enters this prioritization in the offering maps.

It is important not to lose sight of the vision and the goals set for the digital workplace. To relate back to these and ensure that the strategy is developed in the right direction, the working group should ask itself the following questions:

---

45   Alan Smith, Alexander Osterwalder, Gregory Bernarda, Trish Papadakos, and Yves Pigneur, *Value Proposition Design: How to Create Products and Services Customers Want* (Wiley, 2014)

- Will the offerings specified contribute to realizing the vision and goals?
- Is there reason to change the priorities to enable the realization of the vision and goals?
- Is there reason to adapt the vision and goals to new insights gained from working on the user group profiles, needs maps, and offering maps?

The working group should now make an initial sketch of what needs the digital workplace will address and what offerings it will provide. This is where traditional development and design work usually stops. As a result, the user groups' flows of activities and moves between work environments are not properly analyzed and supported. This is why it is important to put the needs and offerings in a more everyday context, which is done with employee journeys.

4.5.8   IDENTIFYING USAGE SITUATIONS

After the working group has created an initial image of what needs the digital workplace should fulfill and how it should do this in the form of offerings, the next step is to validate and supplement the needs and offerings. This is done by linking the needs of the user groups to specific usage situations. Examples include when an employee reads up on what has happened in a project while commuting to work, when an employee writes a status report on a computer at a desk, or when an employee works with other colleagues in the form of a workshop in a meeting room.

Specifying the needs and how they are met in common usage situations enables us to grasp how the digital services are used in practice. If the usage situations are also illustrated, this helps make the future state easier to understand. In addition, they serve as a basis for creating a more coherent user experience from one usage situation to another.

One way to get started is to imagine how a working day might look for an employee belonging to a specific user group once the future state has been achieved:

- When, how, and where does their work begin?
- What situations does the employee work in using what throughout the day?
- Who does the employee collaborate with, and how?
- What is the last thing that happens at the end of the working day?

Figure 60 shows an example of part of an employee journey, which features a specialist at an inspection authority who works in several different situations throughout the day.

Figure 60. Example of an employee journey with different usage situations.

Different usage situations create different conditions for the employees to perform their work:

1. The day starts with commuting to the office, where the specialist takes the opportunity to review new events, plan the working day, and perform simple administrative tasks.
2. At the office, the day continues with a meeting which gathers the members of a distributed project team.

3. The specialist then moves around the office and takes the opportunity to obtain various updates and perform social activities.

4. The specialist then sits down in a part of the office suitable to do more concentrated work and creates a report with a colleague working remotely.

5. During the afternoon, the specialist visits a hospital to inspect whether procedures are in compliance with existing rules.

To gain a better understanding of and describe the conditions in a specific usage situation, the working group fills in a *situation card* (Figure 61).

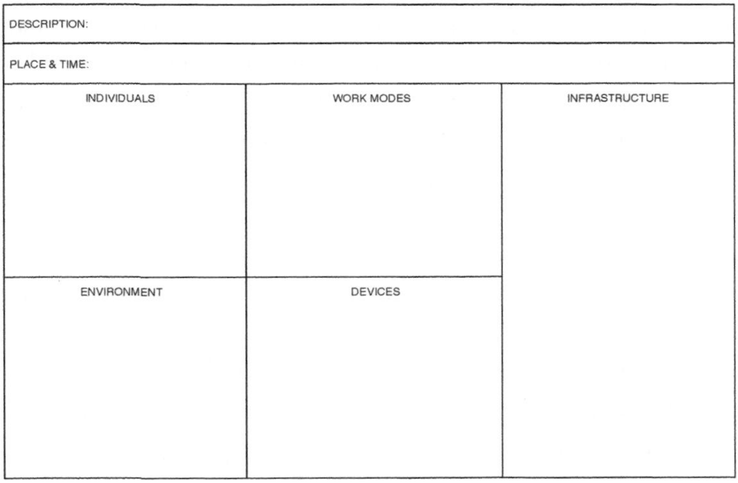

DESCRIPTION:		
PLACE & TIME:		
INDIVIDUALS	WORK MODES	INFRASTRUCTURE
ENVIRONMENT	DEVICES	

Figure 61. Situation card.

The situation card provides a structure for visualizing and pinpointing the conditions and opportunities for the specific usage situation.

Description

The description is a summary of the types of tasks that can be performed in the relevant usage situation. A bus is mainly suitable for individual work or content consumption, less so for participating in meetings or workshops where the idea is to create something with the other participants.

Place and time

Where is the employee, and at what time of day do they perform their work? An example could be on the bus in morning rush-hour traffic.

Individuals

What individuals are around the employee? How many are they, and does the situation dictate interaction with others? There could be many other commuters on the bus who would prefer not to be disturbed by conversation or bulky equipment. Given that the employee may be in close proximity to other people, this situation is not suitable for working on sensitive or classified information either.

Environment

What does the work environment look like? What are the sound levels and lighting conditions? Are there other factors such as temperature, wind, and humidity that could impact working conditions? A bus is in constant motion, which creates a certain degree of instability. This requires that the user is able to maintain a firm grip on their device. The lighting can also vary from dark to bright, which means the screen needs to be protected or angled depending on the angle of the light in the bus.

Work modes

The work mode refers to whether the usage situation is suited for a more forward-leaning position when doing creative work or a more leaned-back position when consuming content. Does it involve short bursts of work or longer periods of productivity and interactivity? If the bus trip lasts 30 minutes and the employee is seated, it may be possible to produce something that requires focus and time. If the employee is standing up on the bus, it is only possible to consume content or perform simple tasks by smartphone.

Devices
What are the conditions for using various digital devices in the relevant usage situation? What can be said about the appropriate size, weight, ways of interacting, suitable media, and the like? If the employee is seated on the bus, a lightweight laptop or tablet could work. If, instead, the employee is standing up, smaller devices such as a smartphone and smartwatch can be used, provided that they support interaction with one hand. Making calls via the device is not appropriate, and audio requires access to headphones or a headset.

Infrastructure
Does the environment contain infrastructure that could facilitate or supplement the use of a device? What does the employee need to interact with services and content effectively? Access to an internet connection and a power supply are basic requirements. For instance, some buses offer a power supply and an internet connection via wireless networks.

4.5.9   COMPOSING EMPLOYEE JOURNEYS

Once the working group has identified and described several typical usage situations with situation cards, it can combine them to compose more coherent employee journeys. The same situation card can be reused several times for the same employee journey and also for several different employee journeys.

A template for describing an employee journey is shown in Figure 62. The template links a specific usage situation to the devices suited to the relevant situation, the activities the employee needs to be able to do, and the services that meet this need.

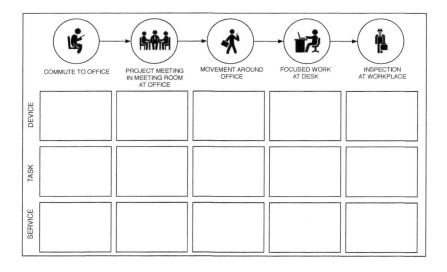

Figure 62. Template for mapping an employee journey.

While working on the outline of the employee journey, the working group might gain new insights into users' needs and the services they use. The employee journey becomes a tool for seeing needs from the employee's day-to-day reality.

The following questions can help in the subsequent assessment of the relevance of an employee journey:

- Does the employee journey reflect reality, that is to say, is the journey relevant and realistic?
- Does the employee journey specify the prioritized needs and capabilities?
- Does the employee journey illustrate a way of working that is in line with business goals?
- Does the scenario depict a modern way of working that empowers employees and makes the most of new digital opportunities?

Once the working group has specified a number of employee journeys, the participants list the most important usage situations that the digital workplace needs to support on the future state canvas. They then do the same for the devices they have determined that the digital workplace needs to support.

4.5.10 ASSESSING THE DELIVERY CAPABILITY

Thus far, the working group has spent quite a lot of time and energy mapping the current state of digital capabilities, digital platforms, and information assets. Now that a vision has been formulated, goals for the future state have been defined, and the needs of the user groups have been made more tangible, we have a comprehensive understanding of the demand. So how should the delivery capability change, and what should it look like in the future state?

Digital capabilities
Starting with the digital capabilities, the working group now has a better idea of what services the user groups need. The current state step included a rough estimate of how effective the digital capabilities are in the current state.

Thus, the working group pulls out the specification of the current digital capabilities and conducts a new assessment of them based on its understanding of the needs of the user groups and the usage situations and devices that need to be supported. This is done by asking the following questions:

- What new or changed digital capabilities are required to meet the needs of each usage situation?
- How should the digital capabilities be prioritized based on prioritized goals and needs?
- If the new needs require changes in ways of working, what digital skills are required?

The same template used to map the digital capabilities in the current state is now used to specify the future state. The prioritization of the digital capabilities in the future state is marked in the future state canvas at the same time as they are listed there.

Digital platforms

A natural follow-up question for the working group is how any changes to the digital capabilities and priorities impact the digital platforms. The questions they now need to ask themselves include:

- Are additional digital platforms needed to provide the capabilities and services prioritized in the canvas?
- Are there important needs and requirements for the characteristics of the services that the current digital platforms struggle to meet?
- Could a better user experience be offered with new or changed digital platforms?

It's easy to get stuck in the complexity lurking behind questions such as these. Therefore, the working group must simply make assumptions and draw conclusions based on the group's collective experience and analytical skills. Strategy development is iterative in nature, and the working group will have reason to return to the same questions in later iterations, most likely with new insights and knowledge.

Information assets

When the working group mapped the needs, it uncovered many examples of what users need to know to perform their tasks. Now the question is how these needs stack up with the information assets in place and how they need to be developed and possibly supplemented.

The working group begins by considering the following questions with the help of the content matrix and notes from the current state:

- Are new information assets required to realize the needs and capabilities of the user groups?
- Do existing information assets need to be supplemented? Can they be made more findable and available? Is their quality in need of improvement?
- Are there new requirements for their content such as improved reusability and portability in their format?

After working through these questions, the working group attempts to summarize what information assets it estimates will be most important to the user groups in the future state. The group then enters the prioritization on the future state canvas.

Now the working group has in its possession a solid basis for creating the first version of the roadmap to realizing the strategy.

4.6   STEP 4 – ROADMAP

Attempting to set a plan that looks several years ahead in a complex world that is also in a constant state of flux may seem contradictory. However, the plan that the working group will create, which we call a roadmap, should be seen as a best possible guess. It can guide the decisions and investments that must be made in any case. It will also be updated regularly as new insights and information emerge during continuing strategy development.

The roadmap in the example below is basically structured from each part of the canvas, but it can, of course, also be broken up in other ways. The model we use is called a fan diagram (Figure 63).

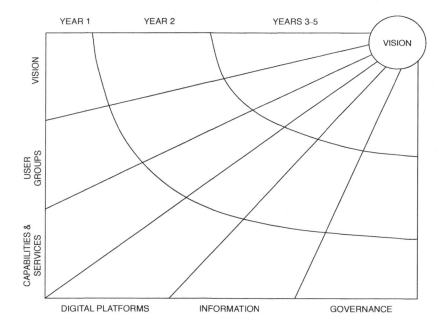

Figure 63. Fan diagram

The structure of the fan diagram makes it possible to show that the activities in the feathers move toward the same future state and eventually toward the vision. As is the case with the canvas, the fan diagram is well-suited for being displayed as a poster, which easily brings people together to discuss the roadmap contents.

Real-world example

In the context of strategy development for a Nordic real estate company, initiatives for capabilities were summarized as shown in Figure 64.

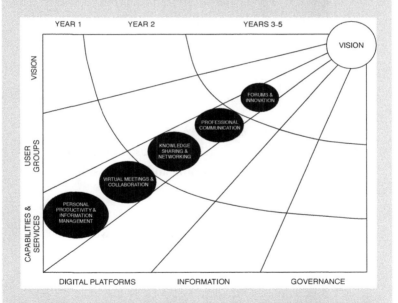

Figure 64. Fan diagram with examples from a real estate company.

The aim was to empower employees with new services and ways of working in a step-by-step manner – from basic capabilities to those more specialized.

The company already had key digital platforms for content management and collaboration in place but wanted to make sure that these platforms were interoperable and used by the employees as intended. This is why they initially focused on reviewing the usability of existing services, facilitating access to them, and ensuring that employees actually used them correctly. They focused on the following domains:

- *Personal productivity and information management* – To make it easier to find content, plan their working day, and share documents.
- *Virtual meetings and collaboration* – To support collaboration and projects in groups, with a focus on shared workspaces and virtual meetings.

In the next step, the company focused on a domain in which it believed there was great business value:

- *Knowledge sharing and networking* – To help employees find each other, make contact, and share information with each other for increased learning and relationship building.

The third step focused on making it easier to work on:

- *Professional communication* – To make it possible for leaders, specialists, and others who want to drive change or are passionate about various issues and subject domains to reach out to, discuss with, and engage colleagues.
- *Forums and innovation* – To give employees the skills to lead, moderate, and develop shared forums, for example, those that bring together colleagues in various areas of interest to share knowledge or ideas with each other.

4.6.1   IDENTIFYING CONTENT FOR THE ROADMAP

The working group now has access to a canvas for the current state, a canvas for the future state, and several identified improvements. In cases where there are differences between the current state and the future state, the gap must be bridged with various actions and initiatives. The roadmap is a tool for organizing these and putting them in chronological order.

The working group now goes through existing documentation, brainstorms ideas and proposals for activities and actions that can bring the organization from the current state to the future state, and then groups them into more coherent initiatives.

> **Real-world example**
>
> The Nordic real estate company came up with proposed actions including a new search engine, access to documents by smartphone, and clear procedures for archiving digital information. These and other related proposed actions were grouped into a more coherent initiative called *Personal Productivity and Information Management*.

Once again, the working group returns to the prioritization matrix to sort which initiatives add the most value in relation to the effort required. They then move these to the fan diagram.

An initiative can sometimes be turned into a project immediately, but the actual design of the project may depend on several factors such as available resources and other ongoing projects. As a result, an initiative sometimes needs to be split into multiple projects, or multiple initiatives may need to be implemented as one project.

There are some simple guidelines for how to place initiatives in the roadmap:

- Initiatives with high value and low effort must come as early as possible in the roadmap.
- Initiatives that involve creating basic conditions are also placed as early as possible in the roadmap.
- If there are special dependencies between initiatives, they need to be placed in the right order in relation to one another in the roadmap.
- If there are initiatives that can pose greater risks, these should be broken down into smaller and more manageable initiatives.

4.6.2   CHECKING THE ROADMAP CONTENTS

The working group now needs to check that the roadmap really contains the right things based on what direction the organization wishes to take. The working group asks itself questions such as:

- Are the most important strategic activities and initiatives in the roadmap?
- Will these initiatives be sufficient to meet the prioritized goals?
- Will the user groups and stakeholders be satisfied if these initiatives are implemented?

To ensure that the initiatives of the roadmap are actually implemented, it is critical to establish an owner of the roadmap. If no owner was identified in the current state step, this done now by asking:

- Who owns and manages the roadmap in its entirety?
- How do we ensure that initiatives are started, followed up, and completed?
- How will the initiatives and the entire change journey, including implementation and change management, be tied together?

If the working group identifies deficiencies in the governance of the digital workplace, then these should be remedied immediately. Ownership of digital services and platforms may be lacking. Or perhaps existing roles and forums are insufficient to steer toward the future state.

Now that an initial version of the digital workplace strategy has been completed, we have a stable foundation in place for the parties involved to gather around and base decisions on. But how do we secure support for the strategy's contents and ensure implementation moves forward?

4.7   STEP 5 – COMPLETION

Digital workplace development revolves around an organization's most important assets – its employees. This is why things tend to come up that enable us to make better use of the organization's talents and resources, add greater value for stakeholders, and create a meaningful and engaging work situation for the employees.

4.7.1   GARNER SUPPORT WITH SEMINARS

To garner further support for the strategy, we recommend conducting one or more seminars with the most important stakeholders of the digital workplace. During the seminars, the working group can both pinpoint and discuss the consequences of the strategy for the organization and obtain crucial input to help improve it. The working group should also present and explain its observations and proposals to the participants.

If it hasn't been done earlier, now is as good a time as any to collect input from a broader range of interested employees. This could involve demonstrations and invitations to read and comment on the entire strategy or else selected parts. If possible, the strategy should be put up in a digital space that also supports the capability to provide feedback.

4.7.2   RUNNING A RETROSPECTIVE

The working group runs a retrospective prior to completing the first iteration of the strategy process. Then it goes over what was effective during strategy development and what could be improved in the next iteration.

Now that the first version of the digital workplace strategy is in place, it's time to begin implementing it.

The next iteration in the development of the strategy begins once again with a start-up phase, but it is much shorter than the first iteration. It may involve changing the composition of the working group, identifying user representatives, and following up on the progress of various initiatives. But this time there is more focus on checking whether something has changed or needs to change since the first iteration.

The working group participants have now begun to get their feet wet. They have gone through the entire strategy process and gained hands-on experience of applying its methods and tools. Now they can focus on additional or deeper work on relevant challenges and issues.

4.8   SUMMARY

In this chapter we covered:

- How to involve the right stakeholders and key personnel to build consensus, provide support both in words and actions, and infuse the change process with energy.

- How to link the digital workplace strategy to other business and IT strategies to secure support for it in significant business goals while relating it to important external trends.

- How to make the strategy comprehensible and rooted in reality with visualizations and outside-in thinking focused on the users.

- How to shape stories and specify usage situations and user journeys in a way that enables decision-makers and users to understand how the change affects them.

- How to pick up on knowledge of practical usage and engage users and ambassadors who are important to the implementation of the strategy.

- How to ensure clear ownership of the strategy in whole and in part, which is a basic prerequisite for making things happen.

- How to show that the strategy is capable of being implemented in specific value-added actions in the short and long term.

- How to take an iterative approach and regularly update the strategy based on new lessons learned and changes in conditions.

- The importance of a common vocabulary, tangible models, and cross-disciplinary teams to ensure a culture of collaboration and increase innovativeness.[46]

What is the right mindset and way of working step by step to gradually develop the digital workplace and the services identified as needed by the organization and employees? We answer this in the next chapter.

---

46 Sarah Gibbons, "Design Thinking Builds Strong Teams," *Nielsen Norman Group*, https://www.nngroup.com/articles/design-thinking-team-building/, (September 18, 2016).

CHAPTER 5

FROM STRATEGY TO DESIGN

5.1   INTRODUCTION

How do we design the digital work environment in practice? We think a coordinated and iterative process for digital service development with high user participation is what's needed. So let's start by looking at some of the most important aspects.

5.1.1   INVOLVING THE USERS IN THE PROCESS

Creating a successful digital service requires building a profound understanding of the intended users and their needs, expectations, and circumstances. Otherwise, it is difficult to come up with the right solution to the right problem. One way of doing this is to directly involve user representatives in the process of developing a service. Having them involved in the process makes it easier for us to understand them, their needs, and their usage situations. There are also other advantages to their involvement:

- They have a natural focus on meeting their own needs, which makes them more inclined to put ideas under the microscope to see whether they truly add value.

- They usually do not have the same knowledge of technical limitations, which enables them to think more freely and outside the box, and thus come up with new ideas.

When developing consumer-centric digital services, it is now a given to involve end users in the development of the service, preferably as early as possible and on a large scale. However, this is far from the norm for digital services geared toward employees even though it is much easier to find and involve employees than consumers for many reasons:

- We know from the outset quite a lot about who they are, what they do, and what situation they are in.

- Employees will likely be interested in participating because it gives them the opportunity to influence their own work situation.

- Securing the employees' time and ensuring they actually can participate are aspects the organization generally has full control over.

Another reason to involve the employees is to ensure that they are capable of adopting the changes that need to be made. Their ability to adopt changes also largely depends on their involvement in the change process and the extent to which they are enabled to influence and prepare for the changes to come. Therefore, we believe that user adoption – the process of users adopting a digital service that works to meet a specific need – begins at the idea stage, not only after a digital service is launched.

Involving employees as intended users is a way of ensuring that the digital service meets their needs in the best way possible and fits well into the digital workplace.

5.1.2   EXPLORING OPPORTUNITIES ITERATIVELY

In a complex and changing world with great uncertainty, we need to be able to quickly test hypotheses on both problems and solutions to figure out whether we are solving the right problem the right way. We cannot analyze our way through this sitting behind a screen at a desk. We must go out into the real world and test our hypotheses and solutions over and over again. This requires an iterative way of working.

An iterative way of working makes experimentation easier and allows us to cope with occasional failure. We can have some select users test an idea or solution at an early stage and at a low cost to see whether or not it has the desired impact. If it doesn't, we can find out why, test another idea, or make necessary changes to the solution and allow the users to test it again.

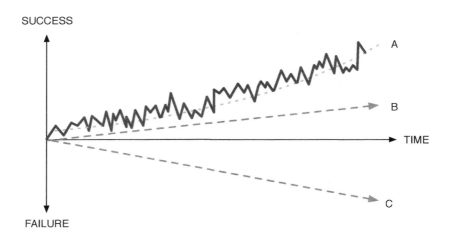

Figure 65. Comparison between an iterative approach and waterfall methodology.

This iterative approach is illustrated by line A in Figure 65. It shows how the way up is not quite straightforward, but failures do not set us back too much either because we always take small, manageable steps.

In contrast, if we employ a development process that is not iterative and, additionally, is not based on a high degree of user involvement, then we will not know whether the final results will have the desired impact until development is complete. The probability of success is also weakened significantly. This is often discovered well after the results (usually a system) have been rolled out to the users and have (hopefully) started to be used in the business. Of course, it may be the case that we make some progress toward the desired impact (line B), but it is also possible that we fail to reach it at all (line C).

Failure late in the process usually means there is no chance to go back and get it right. The time and money allocated have most likely been exhausted or are insufficient for starting over. To avoid them going down the drain, more time and money are often pumped into the system in the hopes that it will improve and begin to generate a return on investment. No one has the courage or resolve to say, "Let's start from scratch and get it right."

The advantages of an iterative approach are thus apparent when it comes to minimizing risks. However, the iterative way of working should still be seen primarily from a value perspective. Working iteratively gives us the opportunity to gradually build an increasing understanding of the intended users, their needs, and other conditions, thus finding the right solutions and designing them the right way.

5.1.3   ESTABLISHING GOVERNANCE AND COORDINATION

Many of the problems that characterize the digital work environments of today – such as fragmentation, unnecessary complexity, and redundancy – can only be solved with better governance and coordination. The first step is to ensure that the digital workplace has an owner who takes responsibility for solving the problems that would otherwise fall between the cracks, or between the silos, if you will.

We also need service owners who are responsible for the services provided within the digital workplace. In this case, the owner of the digital workplace is responsible for ensuring that all digital services share an updated, complete, and effective strategy, a coherent and consistent architecture, and functioning governance and coordination. In turn, the service owners are responsible for their services delivering value to the users and the business and for following the strategy and architecture in place for the digital workplace.

Other domains that span all services include the user experience, service architecture, infrastructure services, and information architecture. These need to inform service development so that each part (service) of the digital workplace is developed in the same direction and adapted to each other, thus avoiding fragmentation, unnecessary complexity, and redundancy.

5.1.4   IMPROVING CONTINUOUSLY

The term "continuous improvement" comes from the Japanese word *Kaizen* and was made famous by Japanese automotive manufacturer Toyota, which has Kaizen as one of its five core values. The point of departure is that no process can ever be completely perfect and, therefore, there is always room for improvement. The same applies to digital services. The digital workplace should be developed as an ongoing process. Instead of making major changes every now and then in a way that neither the business nor the individual employee can cope with, changes should be made all the time. We have illustrated the difference between these two approaches in Figure 66.

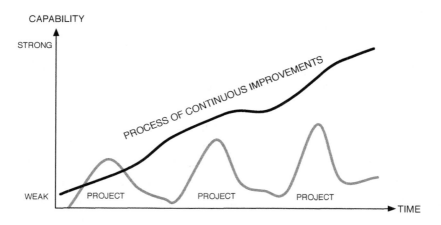

Figure 66. A continuous improvement process strengthens capabilities in the long term.

As prescribed by Toyota's Kaizen approach, change should be a way of life, and everyone in the organization should be involved in the improvement process. As users of the digital services provided within the digital workplace, employees are naturally the greatest source of potential improvement. This makes learning how they use the services, how they experience them, and what they struggle with invaluable for continuously improving the services.

This can be done indirectly through a variety of methods, including everything from surveys and interviews to measurements and observations. However, we could also involve and engage every employee in the change process and get them to actively participate in it, both by providing feedback on how the digital services work and by personally participating in the service development process, which unlocks great improvement potential.

The change process for digital services requires functioning collaboration between the business (in the form of the customers and users) and the service provider. The users have the best view of how the service functions in day-to-day business and what problems may arise. Therefore, the business and service provider must enable the users to provide feedback in order to get a clearer understanding of the users' view.

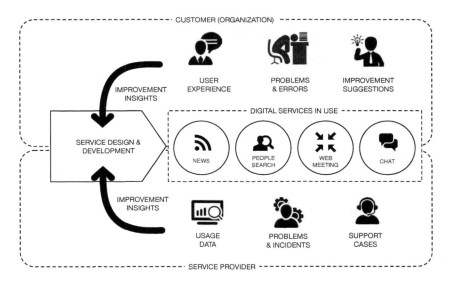

Figure 67. Examples of sources of insight for improvements.

As illustrated by Figure 67, there are many sources from which to gather the insights required for improvements.

Feedback on the user's experience of the services, including the problems and errors they encounter, as well as any suggestions for improvement can provide valuable insights into how the services could be improved. In addition, we naturally have all the usage data that can be collected automatically when users interact with a service.

The service provider's support functions also play a key role in enabling feedback and communicating the information collected and insights obtained to both the service owner and the customers.

5.1.5   DEVELOP EMPATHY FOR INNOVATIVE THINKING

There is nothing worse than doing the wrong thing well.

– Peter F Drucker

People's needs, behaviors, and expectations are in constant flux. The same applies to technology and the possibilities for solving problems. This requires systematic and regular scrutiny to determine what the right solution is and what need should be met. Such a process will hopefully lead to groundbreaking solutions and innovation. Thus, innovation involves not only new technology but also how problems are solved. Sometimes innovation occurs with new technology. Sometimes not. Most innovations emerge from taking existing technology, perhaps from another domain, and composing it in a new way to solve another problem or meet another need. The problem that can be solved or the need that can be met serve as the starting point for all successful innovations.

To be able to solve a problem, you must truly understand it. And truly understanding the problem requires empathy. Empathy involves feeling for and understanding the people who suffer from the problem or who are otherwise involved. If we really do this, we have created a solid foundation from which we can help them and add value. At the same time, if we can learn what opportunities and limitations there are, such as those relating to digital technology, and have the knowledge and skills to make the most of them, then we have everything we need to create something new and better – something truly groundbreaking.

Empathy is the mother of innovation. This also applies to inventions and is surely how the old saying, *Necessity is the mother of invention*, should be interpreted. The farmers who bought their land and experimented to discover more efficient agricultural practices in the 18th century, including shifting from monoculture to crop rotation, probably did this out of a profound understanding of the perilous situation they and their loved ones faced – death by starvation. The innovations did not come from or at the urging of the landowners – they generally had little interest in agriculture.

Rather, the innovations came from those who knew what it meant to starve or were at risk of having to learn what it meant. Empathy is born out of necessity. Luckily, we do not need to risk dying of starvation to develop the empathy required to solve real problems. With a little practice and a variety of methods, we can empathize even with people who are far away, who look and speak differently, and live under completely different circumstances – without being forced to by necessity.

If we are serious about wanting to find and tap the enormous potential that most likely lies within the Internet of Things, virtual reality, artificial intelligence, predictive analysis, and other emerging technologies, we must put much more effort into developing empathy. We need to understand other people and the situations they are in, or risk being in, if we do not do something. Design thinking has an important role to play here, where empathy is crucial and user involvement is a way of ensuring we do not forget about the users or miss out on making the most of their ideas.

Design thinking also provides creative methods and tools for exploring opportunities while gaining a more in-depth understanding of the problems. We need to connect with the people whose problems we want to solve and make the possibilities of technology more accessible to them. If we succeed, we can achieve amazing things – things that really make a difference.

5.1.6   AIMING FOR GROUNDBREAKING IMPROVEMENT

Talking to, listening to, and observing the users is extremely important for developing successful digital services. At the same time, it is not always certain that users understand what they need because they do not see what digital technology enables. Some may think that Steve Jobs was being arrogant when he said, "A lot of times, people don't know what they want until you show it to them". However, in retrospect, we can surely all understand that he had a point. And he was certainly not alone in this insight. Henry Ford, founder of Ford Motor Company, is reputed to have said the following about the Ford Model T:

> *"If I had asked people what they wanted, they would have said faster horses."*

Regardless of whether or not Ford actually said this, we think that these words should not be interpreted as advice to ignore the input of the intended customers or users. Although the users may not be capable of seeing the best solution to meet their needs, they could very well know what they need.

The point is that we should not let ourselves be limited when studying and attempting to understand the employees and their needs based on how they work today. We need to allow ourselves to think outside the box. Digitalization makes it possible to solve problems in ways that are completely or partly new and to address needs, problems, and opportunities that we did not even know existed. These are inconceivable to most employees; therefore, they cannot provide input. Thus, while trying to understand the employees and their needs, we must also ask ourselves if technology and other resources enable new and better ways of achieving the same impact – or a significantly better impact. Otherwise, services like Uber and AirBnB would never have seen the light of day.

There is nothing stopping us from thinking outside the box about the digital workplace and its services as well. Perhaps the key to simplifying the new password process for a user is that he or she does not need a password at all. Therefore, we need to explore these opportunities and also use various hypotheses to challenge employees to think outside the box about their work and how they can achieve a certain goal. As illustrated in Figure 68, a business that wishes to use digitalization to its advantage should aim to use a new technology to enable new ways of working that can lead to groundbreaking improvements.

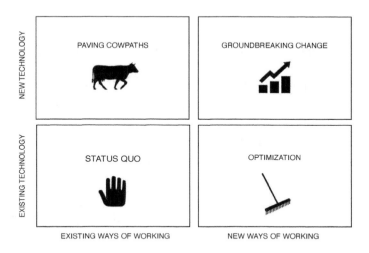

Figure 68. Aim for groundbreaking improvement.

Some may consider it bordering on provocative to propose making hypotheses about solutions before even starting to identify the needs of the business and users. But these hypotheses are needed for gaining inspiration, provoking new ways of thinking, and revealing how digital technology can be used to lighten the load and make things easier for employees. Questions such as, "What work do you do today?" can be supplemented with, "If you had this, how would you have worked?" However, it may take a little time and much testing before a hypothesis can be rejected or scrapped.

Therefore, we want to challenge you and your organization to think outside the box about digital services for employees. Here, innovation must be possible as well, not just for digital services targeting us as consumers. This is an opportunity too good to pass up, but seizing it will require a coordinated, structured, and iterative approach to digital service development – one that enables your organization to identify and explore new digital opportunities that solve the right problems and realize them quickly and effectively.

5.2   PLANNING SERVICE DEVELOPMENT

The digital workplace consists of a number of digital services that are provided for the organization's employees. These services are what the organization gives its employees to support the best ways for them to do their work. This offering should always be as complete as possible. By that, we mean that the employees have access to all the services they need to do their work and add value for customers and the organization.

We gained an overall understanding of the digital workplace's offering during strategy development using user groups and offering maps. This understanding will now be sharpened and detailed during service development. Of course, an organization does not have infinite resources in terms of which and how many digital services it can provide. This necessitates a systematic way of choosing what new services are needed and which existing services will continue to be provided, along with what level of ambition we should have for each service. What we want to avoid most is spending time and money on two or more services that do basically the same thing when we could make one service outstanding instead.

Thus, an important part of digital service development is planning what services need to be provided. The key is to optimize the use of the organization's resources to generate the highest possible value. To do this, we must get a complete view of, and gain control over, all the digital services that are provided or planned to be provided.

However, many businesses lack such a complete view, and consequently, also lack control. The digital work environment often grows organically. Few (if anyone) have a full overview of what is out there, especially if you include shadow IT,[54] the systems and services purchased by different users and business units that are outside the control of the IT department. For example, it's not uncommon for an organization to pay many times for the same or similar services – solely on account of not knowing the service had already been purchased. In part, this is a consequence of focusing on platforms instead of services, which creates redundancy or a gap in the offering. But this is frequently also a consequence of an internal IT department that is unable to quickly meet the needs of the business well, whereby business units see themselves forced to circumvent the IT department and purchase services and systems outside of its control.

5.2.1   THE SERVICE PORTFOLIO

To get a complete picture of and gain control over the digital workplace and services, we recommend building a *service portfolio* that describes the current service range (service catalog), new or changed services that will potentially be introduced (service pipeline), and those that have been phased out and can no longer be delivered (retired services).

---

54 The use of IT-related hardware or software by a department or individual
    without the knowledge of the IT or security group within the organization.

The service portfolio and each of its parts are illustrated conceptually in Figure 69.

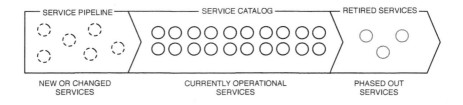

Figure 69. Illustration of service portfolio.

The service portfolio gives us a tool to manage all services within the digital workplace throughout their life cycle, from idea to phase-out. Essentially, this tool is quite simple although it can be implemented in various more or less complex ways. However, it is important to ensure that the service portfolio is complete and updated so that it describes reality and what is planned.

In Figure 70, we illustrate and briefly describe the lifecycle of a service and how this is reflected in the service portfolio.

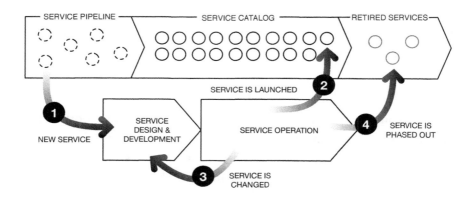

Figure 70. Movement of a service in the service portfolio during its lifecycle.

1. We see the need for a new service, then we specify it and place it in our service portfolio.

2. When the new service is ready, we launch and provide it to the users. It is now included in the existing service range, which is often specified in a service catalog.

3. We change the service as needed. New versions of the service replace the one currently in operation.

4. We phase out the service when we determine it is no longer needed or that it should be replaced with another service for some other reason.

This simple type of overview provided by the service portfolio is highly useful when we wish to obtain a holistic view of the digital workplace. It enables changes to be planned and coordinated without having to go into too much detail.

5.2.2   THE SERVICE CATALOG

An organization should view the digital workplace and its services the same way a company views its offering to the market and its customers. In chapter 2, we used the example of a restaurant where the menu is usually the first thing we want to see to determine whether there is something that meets our needs and preferences as well as what it costs. If there's no menu, how will customers find something that meets their needs?

The existing service range should be specified in a service catalog, which can be considered equivalent to the restaurant menu. Just like the menu, the service catalog should quickly give every stakeholder a uniform, complete, and up-to-date view of what is offered within the scope of the digital workplace.

If we continue to use the restaurant analogy and consider those which are best at describing and communicating what they offer, then these are often fast food restaurants (as they want us to make up our minds and order quickly). The choices on offer are usually clearly described with images and text that include key characteristics. They also offer meals that meet various typical needs and preferences. Thus, many can order what they want directly without having to make too many choices. We can think along the same lines when specifying and communicating the service range of the digital workplace. In Figure 71, we show a select few examples of what a service catalog could contain.

Figure 71. Examples of services in a service catalog.

The employees need to be able to quickly understand what's available and find the digital services they need. An example of how to make this easier is for each service to be displayed with a name, an icon, a description of what it is used for, what functionality it contains, and screenshots showing what it looks like. We may also need to specify what prerequisites are required and how to order and gain access to it. To facilitate findability in the service catalog, services may need to be grouped into various categories, especially if there are many services.

With the experience we all have today as users of digital technology and digital services outside of work, it's not difficult to imagine what a service catalog might look like in practice. Just take a look at Apple's App Store or Google Play. An equivalent store should be available for the digital workplace where we can find, order, and gain access to digital services provided in a uniform manner – regardless what service it is and who provides it. For example, it may be relevant to know what services colleagues with similar roles or tasks use, which services are used the most within the organization, and which services other colleagues recommend.

Another advantage of the mobile app analogy is that they are usually more task-centric than traditional websites and systems, making it easier for users to see a specific purpose and value. This is due to the screen space limitations of mobile devices and the fact that mobile devices are suited for usage situations where we want to perform a specific task quickly. Therefore, we will return to the app analogy.

However, the offering to employees not only involves the individual services specified in the service catalog but also includes what characteristics the digital workplace needs to have and how it should be experienced as a whole. The digital work environment is the sum of each and every system and service we use in our work. As described in chapter 1, we must address the problems that result in productivity losses for the business and that result in stress and illness on the part of employees. We do this by designing the digital work environment purposefully and ensuring that, as a whole, it is as simple, coherent, flexible, and consistent as possible, with the least possible redundancy and the highest possible usability. We cannot begin to talk about the digital workplace until we work purposefully in this direction.

So, is there such a thing as typical services in a digital workplace? Definable and repeatable business processes are often supported by various enterprise systems. Employees of an organization's finance department surely use an enterprise system that provides services such as order management, purchasing, invoicing, and accounting. But what services are needed depends to a great degree on the scope and nature of the business.

Each enterprise system and its services can be seen as more or less isolated islands in the digital work environment, as the services are intended to support different parts of the business. To be more productive, agile, and innovative, an organization must also provide digital services that enable communication and collaboration between employees across the entire business.

Traditionally, many organizations have been poor at providing these types of services – those that should be at the heart of the digital workplace around which all other services revolve. Therefore, let's use these as an example of typical services required in a digital workplace.

Today, services for enterprise-wide communication and collaboration are usually made available via an organization's intranet and various communication tools. For example, if we look at what most traditional intranets consist of, we can see the following main components:

- A newsfeed with news geared toward employees.

- A search function that enables searches of the content on the intranet's pages and documents.

- Information pages describing various parts of organizations and the business, including everything from the organization's values, vision, and management to practical information in domains such as human resources, finance, and IT.

- A catalog of information about employees, including everything from their role, organizational affiliation, and contact information to interests and expertise.

- Links to various web-based tools and systems that employees need to do their work and perform administrative tasks.

5.3   SERVICE DESIGN

For most organizations, it is a major challenge to improve the digital work environment and create a digital workplace in which the employees thrive and are productive. One key is to give employees access to the right services designed in the right way. This is where concepts such as design thinking and service design come into play.

In design thinking, as previously addressed, we start with a user perspective, attempt to understand the user's needs or problems, and experiment until we find the best possible solution using various types of prototypes. Service design starts with the approach and methods of design thinking in order to design a service in such a way that it gives the user the best possible experience. However, we must provide services that are not only useful and appealing to use but also add the desired business value and are technically feasible (Figure 72).

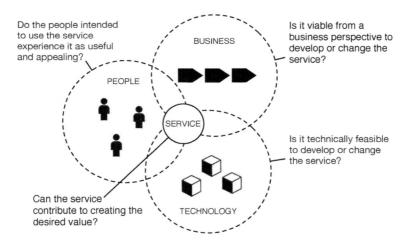

Figure 72. Service design combines knowledge about users, business, and technology.

In addition to design skills, succeeding in this will require knowledge and skills in all three of the perspectives: user, business, and technology.

These must be available throughout the process of developing a service, which normally means that people with this knowledge and these skills need to participate in the development of the service.

Service design creates a holistic view of the service: all interactions the user has with the service – via all touchpoints – are considered in its design. This can be compared with interaction design and user interface (UI) design, which focus on the interaction in a single touchpoint, such as between the user and a mobile app. Marc Stickdorn highlights five principles that distinguish service design: user-centered, holistic, co-creative, sequencing, and evidencing, which we describe in brief below.[55]

User-centered
A user-centered approach involves attempting to develop a more in-depth understanding of and empathy for the intended user and what this user needs and values. This is made easier by attempting to experience the service through the lens of the user to the greatest degree possible. Service design gives us a wide variety of methods for doing this.

Holistic
To develop a service correctly, we must first understand the context in which it is used. This is also very much the case for digital services. The point of departure should be that everything impacting the experience of a service must be considered in the design of the service. Zooming out and seeing the bigger picture makes it easier to understand the usage situations the user is in, what problems and challenges the user could encounter, and what thoughts and feelings impact usage of the service.

Co-creative
Co-creation, or co-creative design, is a key term in service design. We must involve people with a wide variety of skills, perspectives, and experience to find the right problem and solve it correctly. In service design, we tackle this challenge by working together in multi-disciplinary teams in which the customer and user also participate.

---

55 Marc Stickdorn and Jacob Schneider, *This is Service Design Thinking: Basics, Tools, Cases* (Wiley, 2012).

Sequencing

Sequencing means that the service is visualized as a sequence of related activities over time. For knowledge work, it may be difficult to identify and specify repeatable processes, but sequencing is still useful because it makes it possible to identify and understand typical workflows and design services to support them.

Evidencing

Showing how a user will experience a digital service before it is complete can be difficult. To pull it off anyway, we must make the service tangible as early as possible, which is usually done with various types of prototypes and by allowing the user to interact with it and test it in as realistic usage contexts as possible.

5.3.1   THE SERVICE DESIGN PROCESS

What does a typical service design process look like? To put it simply, service design is about understanding the prospective user and their needs, problems, and challenges, identifying various hypotheses about how these needs can be met, and testing various solutions with users without having to fully realize them. The process for doing this can be divided into several steps, as illustrated in Figure 73.

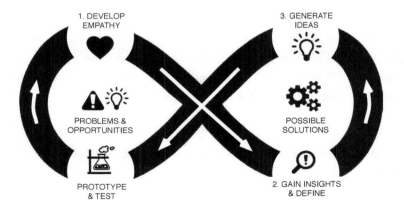

Figure 73. The service design process

The illustration shows that this is no linear process where each step and the process as a whole are only implemented once. The service design process revolves around two questions we return to time and time again:

1. What problem is the right problem to solve?
2. What is the best way to solve it?

We constantly move back and forth between these questions, but as we repeat the process, the problems we need to solve become clearer and our focus increasingly shifts toward the question of how to solve them. One iteration can generally be made in one week – and sometimes even during one workshop.

Next, we briefly go over the purpose of each step in the service design process and give some examples of methods that are useful. We have selected an existing digital service in need of development or change and assembled a team consisting of service designers, relevant subject matter experts, and IT specialists.

1. Developing empathy
The purpose of the empathy step is to identify and understand the prospective users as well as possible, including their tasks and usage situations. We also map the business and the technology available in order to understand these and other possibilities and limitations we must consider. There are many useful methods we can use in this step of the process, and we will now go through some of those most useful for the development of services for the digital workplace.

Interviews
Interviewing one or more people from a user group enables us to build an understanding of the needs and circumstances of the relevant user group. Interviews can also be used to uncover how users experience a service in order to evaluate the service in question and identify potential for improvement.

Focus groups

Focus groups are suitable when we want to find out what values, motives, preferences, and needs characterize individuals in a specific target group. They are useful in the initial stage for building knowledge of the user groups and their needs and expectations.

Journals

Asking employees to keep journals of when they use a service or perform their tasks is a way of collecting their experiences of the service or their work situation. The journal may take a number of forms and could even include having the employee take pictures and record videos of their working day.

Field studies

A field study entails following one or more employees as they work in their natural work environment. This enables us to gain an understanding of the employees, their tasks and work environment, as well as how they use and experience digital services in their work.

Task analysis

A task analysis aims to understand what specific tasks an employee must perform to achieve their goals and what steps the employee takes to perform the task. When possible, we draw a process diagram of the workflow and note the problems and deficiencies we have heard of or observed.

Data analysis

In the case of the digital services that employees already use, we can collect data about their behavior, analyze it, and draw conclusions that we can use to improve the service or ask new questions and seek more answers. For example, if we see in the usage statistics for a service that users suddenly stop using it when they reach a certain step, we might want to find out why. Interviews are one way of doing this.

2. Gaining insights and defining

During this step, we analyze the information we have collected using a variety of methods and compile the insights we have gained. To make them applicable in our work to come, the insights must be packaged appropriately, such as by creating personas and user journeys.

A *persona* is a fictitious character who represents a user group and helps give the user group an identity. Therefore, a persona should have the characteristics most representative of the relevant user group. The user profiles created during strategy development serve as a basis here, and with the information collected during the empathy stage, we can create personas with characteristics such as background, role, motivation, interests, and skills. Then we can discuss how the imaginary person would react in certain situations and what needs and preferences this person might have. Thus, a persona should be as real as possible, with a name and picture to give the impression of a real person.

A *user journey*, also referred to as an employee journey in the case of the digital workplace, is a visual process specification that outlines a specific user interaction with a digital service in order to achieve the user's goal. It specifies all the touchpoints where the user interacts with the service and the relationships between these touchpoints. This gives us a good understanding of how each part of the service should interrelate and enables a smoother transition between touchpoints. User journeys focus on the exchange of information between the user and the service and through what devices the interaction occurs. The degree of detail is intentionally not particularly high, as the purpose is rather, through simplification, to gain an understanding and holistic view of the user's process and experience in interaction with the service.

User journeys are often used to map how an existing service is used and to identify any problems and potential for improvement based on how the user actually uses and experiences the service. For example, we employed user journeys in the strategy chapter to visualize the future state and make it tangible.

3. Generating and selecting ideas

The purpose of the idea generation step is to identify potential for improvement to a service. Thus, we gather people with a wide range of knowledge and experience to generate ideas with the help of techniques such as brainstorming and mind maps. We attempt to generate as many ideas as possible for the most important needs, problems, and opportunities we previously identified. As explained earlier, it is extremely valuable here to involve the intended users in the process. We then choose the best ideas to continue working on with the help of a suitable prioritization method. For example, we can see what value the ideas could potentially provide to the business and users, and how much effort is required to realize each idea. We then choose those with a high potential value. It's often wise to begin with the low-hanging fruit among these, that is to say, those that require little effort to realize (Figure 74).

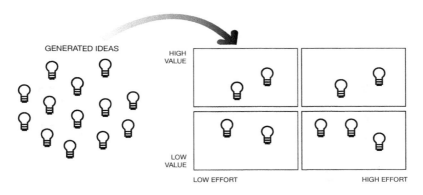

Figure 74. Prioritization matrix for choosing ideas to continue working on.

4. Prototyping and testing solutions

Now we begin to conceptualize the selected ideas using relevant methods and test them on users. For instance, we could use scenarios for sequencing and paper prototypes for evidencing. These help us quickly build an understanding of how the service might function once it is finished although we are relatively far from a finished service.

We use prototyping to evaluate and test the service's design, functionality, and content before it is fully realized. This could be anything from simple paper prototypes to nearly fully developed digital services. Which prototype we decide to create should be primarily determined by what we seek to learn when testing it with users. If we wish to test whether a certain workflow works, perhaps it is not so important to have a realistic prototype, as a series of paper sketches (paper prototypes) or a presentation would be sufficient.

Generally speaking, the earlier you begin prototyping to make an idea or hypothesis tangible, the faster you can evaluate the idea to determine whether it is sound and what could be improved. We want to learn how the concepts we have created work, what is good and bad, what could be improved, what is missing, or what should be removed. We do this by testing the prototypes we have created on prospective users (Figure 75).

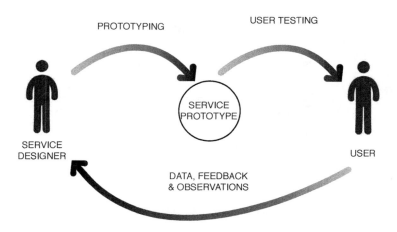

Figure 75. Prototyping and user testing,

Based on the findings of the tests and the conclusions we draw from the analysis, we change what needs to be changed, refine or discard certain elements, and come up with a well-functioning concept with the help of the users. We strive to conduct the tests in as realistic usage situations as possible, which may require that we create more realistic prototypes that share much similarity with the finished service in terms of appearance and functionality.

5.3.2   VALIDATING SOLUTIONS WITH THE LEAST EFFORT

To avoid spending time and money on the wrong things, we want to validate as quickly as possible whether the service we are developing or changing solves the right problems, and if so, how well it solves them. Therefore, we should have employees start using the service in the business as soon as possible. This is done with a minimum viable product (MVP), which is a product with the exact minimum possible functionality and characteristics required for the task while still adding value.

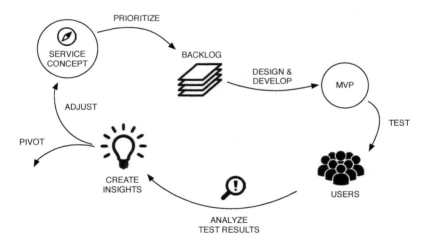

Figure 76. Process from service concept to MVP.

As shown in Figure 76, we first choose what functions and characteristics the MVP should include based on a list of all functions and characteristics we identified for the service, the *backlog*. We realize these and then allow a group of users to test the MVP. Their feedback on what works well or not so well and what they experience as valuable or less valuable gives us insights on what we need to change. Then we continue to further refine the service in upcoming iterations.

One common approach is to introduce early versions of a service to a select group of users for a limited period of time, a pilot period. Once the service is considered good enough, it is launched to all intended users and then refined in a continual service improvement process.

You may be wondering what the difference is between a prototype and an MVP. Well, an MVP is an early version of a digital service that can be trialed and helps us begin collecting data about usage whereas prototypes can be used to collect feedback from users and make observations. However, with prototypes, it is difficult to obtain data from many users about when, where, and how they actually use the service IRL. This data can give us valuable insights about how the service should be designed, and that is why it is important to come up with an MVP quickly.

5.4   MEASURING PROGRESS

To measure is to know, as the saying goes. And there is a lot of truth to another saying, *If you can't measure it, you can't improve it.*

But most of all, it is important to understand why we should measure something. What do we seek to achieve? What goals do we have, and what impact do we want to create? Here, we have our impact objectives to fall back on to determine what we need to measure. The measurability of the objectives is what makes it possible to demonstrate what impact and value has or hasn't resulted from a certain change.

Some impact objectives can be measured by collecting data on how users use the digital service, while others may require the use of surveys and other methods of measurement. This requires measuring before the change has been made as well as measuring regularly afterwards. Given that service development should be seen as a process that is ongoing throughout the life of the service, we need to regularly measure how well the service is performing and meeting the impact objectives.

Usually, it is relatively easy to define measurable impact objectives for a service. Some are easier to measure while others are harder, but nothing is really impossible to measure.

Also, when developing digital services, "carpet bombing" with various measurements lays the foundation for being able to discern patterns later and discover new ways of measuring that we perhaps would not have thought of without having seen the data generated first. Therefore, we recommend measuring as much as possible, while also being very meticulous and selective about what we choose to follow up – we must really know what the data should be used for and understand what it shows.

5.5   PUTTING DESIGN AT THE CORE

Transitioning from traditional IT development to a coordinated and iterative process for digital service development with high user involvement is not something you can do with the simple wave of a wand. In particular, it requires a substantial transfer of skills. So, why should we make this transition? Let's take a look at how design developed from being something that sells products to a business strategy now used by world-leading companies.

Basically, design involves creating something that meets the needs of the users. That is to say, the needs of the intended users of a product or service. If an organization meets the needs of the users well enough, they will want to pay for the product or service. They become the organization's customers. This is how customers and markets are created. Succeeding in meeting someone's needs, preferably better than others, is the foundation of every business. Those who have some other idea, like that the most important thing is maximizing dividends to the owners, are sorely mistaken.

Design is not something that can be added later like an afterthought or that can be delegated to individual specialists. Design is the most powerful tool an organization can wield in its quest for success in a changing world. Design is a business strategy.

The capability to meet needs in new and better ways can, in turn, be summarized with another word – innovation. However, in most "mature" organizations, existing practices win out over innovation any day of the week if they go head-to-head. Following the rules is more important than breaking old rules and making new ones. Upholding is more important than changing. But they cannot continue like this – literally. The only organizations that can survive in the long term are innovative organizations, and they cannot be innovative without design.

Therefore, it is only natural that an increasing number of organizations are developing an interest and striving to build up their capability in design thinking. Design thinking can be seen as an iterative and creative approach where people with various skills and perspectives join together to solve problems and discover new possibilities. At the heart of this is understanding and empathizing with the users and their needs. Because, as mentioned, empathy is the mother of innovation.

Design thinking is not primarily about learning to use a design tool or working under any specific process. It's about learning to think like a designer. We are convinced that we all can and must become designers. Our ability to create things is what distinguishes the human race from other animals. We are all born creative, and although much of our creativity is chipped away when we are squeezed through the education system, design is still in our blood.

Therefore, we should not be too concerned with robots and artificial intelligence taking over part of our work. Let them do the boring, repetitive work for us. Let them help us make better decisions. Then we humans can focus instead on awakening and developing our inherent and uniquely human capabilities, such as empathy, improvisation, collaboration, curiosity, and creative problem-solving.

The digital workplace of tomorrow must help support these qualities, use new technology to give us better capabilities, and unleash the power that arises when many people work closely together toward a common goal.

5.6   SUMMARY

In this chapter we covered:

- Why organizations need a common and coordinated service design process that involves the intended users, is iterative, and encourages experimentation that can lead to groundbreaking innovation and continuous improvements.
- How service development can be planned and coordinated with tools such as a service portfolio, service pipeline, and service catalog.
- A typical service design process and how principles and tools from design thinking and service design can be used to design services that solve the right problems in the right way.

EPILOGUE

"The role of a leader is not to come up with all the great ideas. The role of a leader is to create an environment in which great ideas can happen."

– Simon Sinek

Over the years, we have worked with many organizations, both public and private, in various industries and of varying sizes. We assisted in the development of the digital workplace and digital customer experience, helping our clients digitalize their business. In this book, we have presented the way of working that we jointly developed over these years, as applied to the digital workplace.

We want to conclude by sharing some reflections and insights we gained from our work and by giving you a few additional tips to use in your digital workplace efforts.

The similarities between organizations are often striking in terms of digitalization and what challenges they face. The greatest challenge we can see is the need to embrace and adopt new ways of thinking and working. An approach to digitalization that is iterative, exploratory, inclusive, holistic, value-centric, and user-centered is often at odds with existing structures and ways of working. Organizational silos, groupthink, inside-out thinking, organic and mostly uncontrolled digital work environments, and the difficulty in changing well-established ways of working, attitudes, and behaviors are the most common obstacles.

To overcome these obstacles, top management must have the insight, will, and courage to change existing structures and ways of working. This is rarely the case. Instead, we find that digitalization is often led by a few enthusiastic individuals who champion digitalization in their organizations.

We are pleased that so many people have embraced the way of working and methodology we present in this book. We are especially glad when we learn that the book is actually being used and not just put away on a shelf or forgotten in a digital folder. That was precisely our goal – to provide a pragmatic and proven way of working and a methodology for developing the digital workplace.

To support you in your efforts, we would like to offer you the opportunity to join a Slack group, where you will have access to the models and templates we go through in the book in digital format so you can apply them in your organization. If you're looking for real-world examples of the digital workplace canvas and other tools from the book, this is where you will find them. You will also have the opportunity to meet like-minded professionals, share experiences and tips, and take part in discussions. If you would like to give feedback on the book or anything else, or simply discuss something with us, we are just a click or a tap away.

To join the Slack group, all you need to do is register at **dwstrategydesign.com** – see you there!

We hope this book and the materials you gain access to via the Slack group will help you and your organization create a digital workplace and employee experience that truly empowers people.

Good luck!

Henrik Gustafsson and Oscar Berg

*"The best way
to predict the future
is to create it."*

– Peter F. Drucker

REFERENCES

Albanesi, S.,Gregory, V., Patterson, C., & Şahin, A. (2013) *Is Job Polarization Holding Back the Labor Market?*. Liberty Street Economics,. Retrieved from http://libertystreeteconomics.newyorkfed.org/2013/03/is-job-polarization-holding-back-the-labor-market.html.

Aldag, R. Kuzuhara, L. (2015). *Creating High Performance Teams: Applied Strategies and Tools for Managers and Team Members*. Routledge.

Brinkley, I., Fauth, R., Mahdon, M. & Theodoropoulou, S. (2009). *Knowledge Workers and Knowledge Work - A Knowledge Economy Programme Report*. The Work Foundation. Retrieved from http://www.theworkfoundation.com/assets/docs/publications/213_know_work_survey170309.pdf

Chui, M., Manyika, J., Bughin, J., Dobbs, R., Roxburgh, C., Sarrazin, H., Sands, G., Westergren, M. (2012). *The social economy: Unlocking value and productivity through social technologies*. McKinsey Global Institute. Retrieved from http://www.mckinsey.com/insights/high_tech_telecoms_internet/the_social_economy

Conner, M. L. Clawson, J.G. (2004). *Creating a Learning Culture: Strategy, Technology, and Practice*. Cambridge University Press. Retrieved from http://assets.cambridge.org/052153/7177/excerpt/0521537177_excerpt.pdf

Ditmore, J. (2013). *Why Do Big IT Projects Fail So Often?* InformationWeek. Retrieved from http://www.informationweek.com/strategic-cio/executive-insights-and-innovation/why-do-big-it-projects-fail-so-often/d/d-id/1112087

Drucker, P. F. (1991). *The New Productivity Challenge*. Harvard Business Review. Retrieved from https://hbr.org/1991/11/the-new-productivity-challenge/ar/1

Erl, T. (2005). *Service-Oriented Architecture: Concepts, Technology, and Design*. Prentice Hall.

Elephant and the blind men. (2016). Jainism Global Resource Center. Retrieved from http://www.jainworld.com/literature/story25.htm

Eliel Saarinen. (2016). Quotes on Design. Retrieved from https://quotesondesign.com/eliel-saarinen/

Ergonomics of human-system interaction -- Part 210: Human-centred design for interactive systems. (2015). ISO 9241-210:2010. Retrieved from http://www.iso.org/iso/catalogue_detail.htm?csnumber=52075

Gardner, J.R., Rachlin, R. and Sweeny, HWA (1986). *Handbook of strategic planning*. John Wiley & Sons Inc.

Garfield, S. (2016). *Employee engagement in the Digital Workplace.* Linkedin. Retrieved from https://www.linkedin.com/pulse/employee-engagement-digital-workplace-symon-garfield

Gavett, G. Berinato, S. (2013). *Map: The Sad State of Global Workplace Engagement*. Harvard Business Review. Retrieved from https://hbr.org/2013/10/map-the-sad-state-of-global-workplace-engagement

Gibbons, S. (2016). *Design Thinking Builds Strong Teams*. Nielsen Norman Group. Retrieved from https://www.nngroup.com/articles/design-thinking-team-building/

Godin, S. (2014). *Turning passion on its head.* Seth´s blog. Retrieved from http://sethgodin.typepad.com/seths_blog/2014/08/turning-passion-on-its-head.html

Gray, D. Brown, S. Macanufo, J. (2010). *Gamestorming: A Playbook for Innovators, Rulebreakers and Changemakers*. O'Reilly Media

IT Adoption Insight Report. (2012). Neochange. Retrieved from http://www.ltc4.org/Resources/Documents/Neochange%202012%20 Adoption%20Insight%20Report_v2.pdf

Johnston, L. D. (2012). *History lessons: Understanding the decline in manufacturing*. Minnpost. Retrieved from https://www.minnpost.com/macro-micro-minnesota/2012/02/history-lessons-understanding-decline-manufacturing

Kelly, K. (2017), *The Inevitable: Understanding the 12 Technological Forces That Will Shape Our Future*, Penguin Book

Larsson, L. (2016). *"Advokatrobotar" gör det billigare och lättare att få juridisk hjälp.* DN. Retrieved from http://www.dn.se/nyheter/sverige/advokatrobotar-gor-det-billigare-och-lattare-att-fa-juridisk-hjalp/

Le Clair, C. (2011). *Best Practices: Developing an ECM/BPM strategy.* Forrester. Retrieved from http://www.calcet.com/hyland/Best%20 Practices%20for%20Developing%20an%20ECM%20BPM%20 Strategy%20(2).pdf

Mills-Scofield, D. (2013). *Control Is for Beginners*. Harward Business Review. Retrieved from https://hbr.org/2013/11/control-is-for-beginners

Nobel, C. (2011). *Clay Christensen's Milkshake Marketing*. Harvard Business School. Retrieved from http://hbswk.hbs.edu/item/clay-christensens-milkshake-marketing

Oklarheter kring den digitala arbetsmiljön. (2015). Arbetsmiljöverket. Retrieved from https://www.av.se/press/oklarheterkringden-digitala-arbetsmiljon/

Osterwalder, A. (2010). *Business Model Generation: A Handbook for Visionaries, Game Changers, and Challengers*. John Wiley and Sons

Osterwalder, A. Pigneur, Y. Bernarda, G. Smith A. Papadakos, T. (2014). *Value Proposition Design: How to Create Products and Services Customers Want*. Wiley

Rafati, S. (2015). *What Steve Jobs taught executives about hiring*. Fortune. Retrieved from http://fortune.com/2015/06/09/shahrzad-rafati-keeping-your-best-employees/

Ross, M. (2015). *AP's 'robot journalists' are writing their own stories now*. The Verge. Retrieved from http://www.theverge.com/2015/1/29/7939067/ap-journalism-automation-robots-financial-reporting

Rozwell, C. Aggarwal, A. (2015). *Attention to Eight Building Blocks Ensures Successful Digital Workplace Initiatives*. Gartner

Sager, M. (2007). *Andy Grove: What I've Learned*. Esquire. Retrieved from http://www.esquire.com/entertainment/interviews/a1449/learned-andy-grove-0500/

Schmidt, E. Rosenberg, J. (2014). *How Google Works*. John Murray

Search and Discovery – Exploiting Knowledge, Minimizing Risk. (2014). aiim. Industry Watch. Retrieved from http://www.aiim.org/Resources/Research/Industry-Watches/2014/2014_Sept_Search-and-Discovery

Shirky, C. (2009). *Here Comes Everybody: The Power of Organizing Without Organizations*. Penguin Books

Söderström, J. (2011). *Jävla skitsystem!* Jonas Söderström

Söderström, J. (2015). *Digital arbetsmiljö.* Arbetsmiljö, Vision. Retrieved from http://www.slideshare.net/Jonas_inUse/arbetsmiljoombud-vision-gteborg-8-okt-2015

Stickdorn, M. Schneider, J. (2012). *This is Service Design Thinking: Basics, Tools, Cases.* Wiley

Suarez, L. (2013): *Life Without eMail – 5th Year Progress Report – The Community, The Movement.* elsua. Retrieved from http://www.elsua.net/2013/05/06/life-without-email-5th-year-progress-report-the-community-the-movement/

Westerman, G. Bonnet, D. McAfee A. (2014). *Leading Digital: Turning Technology Into Business Transformation.* Harvard Business Review Press

INDEX

U

unstructured content 32
usability 32
usability deficiencies 32
usage context 140, 197
usage pattern 75
usage process 78
usage situation 71, 73, 79, 103, 126,
    154, 159, 202
user 65
user adoption 179
user-centered 45, 52, 196
user-centric approach 50
user experience 33, 44, 66, 71, 156
user experience debt 33
user group 103, 123, 154
user group profile 125, 154
user involvement 178, 205
user journey 78, 200
user representative 107, 178
user research 106
user segment 123
user-supporting role 107
user testing 201
utility-centric 67

V

value 66
value focus 51
value proposition 21
value proposition canvas 158
vision 48, 95, 103, 116, 150, 169

W

web meeting 79, 85
web page 137
W. Edward Deming 35
work environment 28
work environment problem 33
workflow capabilities 129

workflow management 134
working group 105
working style 123
work mode 74, 162
    74
workshop 100
World Bank 59

PRAISE FOR THE BOOK

Digital Workplace Strategy & Design is a rare combination in a single work of both strategic and pragmatic insights and guidance. I strongly recommend that digital workplace project teams invest the time to read and discuss the book together. The time will be well spent, bringing team members with complementary skills to a shared understanding of how to make the digital workplace the heart of where people interact and create value.

– Jane McConnell, workplace strategy advisor

With diagrams, examples, quotes, and case studies, this book gives a comprehensive view of why the digital workplace is critical to all employees and how organizations need to adopt the right approach. It is a book that you can come back to for specific sections to refresh your memory after absorbing the learning from your initial reading of this book. I wish I had Digital Workplace Strategy & Design with me when I first started my career and benefit from Oscar and Henrik's combined wisdom each working day. However you can do that by reading this book and changing your organization's approach!

– Mark Morrell, intranet pioneer

This is for right-minded people…Some out there prefer doing things by the textbook. Oscar and Henrik deliver the one for your digital workplace journey - but it comes with a disclaimer: it only works if you really believe in it. Delivering empowerment to people at work is way more than designing the amazing IT systems. It's about leading the way into a new age of productivity, togetherness and WE thinking from day one. If you believe you have the stamina for this magnitude of change, make this book yours. It's worth it.

– Philipp Rosenthal, digital business coach at digital-sherpa.me